Let All Within Us Praise!

Dramatic Resources for Worship

Patricia J. Shelly

FAITH & LIFE
P R E S S

Newton, Kansas
Winnipeg, Manitoba

Printed in the United States of America.

International Standard Book Number 0-87303-208-X
Library of Congress Number 96-84113

Editorial direction by Susan E. Janzen; editing by Eddy Hall; copyediting by Mary L. Gaeddert; design by Gwen Stamm; printing by Mennonite Press, Inc. Cover design by Gwen Stamm.

In memory of my father and first pastor,
Rev. Kenneth Myers Shelly (1930-1994),
who first taught me the joy of worship

And to the students, faculty, and staff
of the Bethel College chapel community—
"How Can We Keep from Singing?"

Contents

Acknowledgments

An Invitation

Part I: Using Readers Theater in Worship 1

Part II: Dramatic Readings 7

With Heart, Soul, Mind, and Strength

  1. With Thankful Hearts 10

  2. With All Your Soul 13

  3. Treasuring God's Wisdom 16

  4. With All Your Strength 19

  5. If You Do This, You Will Live 22

Let All Within You Praise

  6. A Modern Psalm: Call to Praise 26

  7. Bless the Lord, O My Soul 28

  8. Know and Serve the Lord with Gladness 31

  9. Declare God's Marvelous Works 34

10. God Is Our Refuge and Strength 37

11. How Can We Sing in a Strange New Land? 40

12. Lord, You Have Searched Me 43

13. Two Worlds of Experience 46

14. A Cry from the Depths 48

15. Through the Valley of the Shadow 51

16. Responsive Reading on Psalm 23 and the Beatitudes 54

Old Testament Readings

17. What Do These Stones Mean? 58

18. Micah 6: A Dramatic Paraphrase 61

19. Seek the Lord: Micah and the Prophets 64

20. Behold! I Make All Things New 68

21. A Heart of Wisdom 71

The Parables of Matthew 13

22. What Is New, What Is Old 76

23. Parable of the Sower 79

24. Mystery and Growth 83

25. Weeds and Harvest 86

Gospel Readings

26. The People Who Walk in Darkness 90

27. Ancient Advent Songs 93

28. A Perceptive Story 97

29. Ask, Seek, Knock 102
30. A Thanksgiving Reading 106
31. "Who Am I?" The Suffering One, The Transfigured One 109
32. Christ as King and Christ as Servant 111
33. The Spirit of God (Reading 1) 114
34. The Spirit of God (Reading 2) 116
35. With Thanksgiving 119

Readings from Paul

36. Parable of the Body 124
37. Present Your Bodies a Living Sacrifice 127
38. Christ Is Our Peace (Reading 1) 129
39. Christ Is Our Peace (Reading 2) 132
40. Ministry of Reconciliation 134
41. The Breadth and Length and Height and Depth 137
42. Awake, Rise, and Christ Will Shine on You 140

Other Resources

43. God Is Our Song 144
44. An Undaunted Divine Comedy 147
45. Benediction 151

Part III: Songs 153

1. Love the Lord (With All) 156
2. Philippian Hymn 160
3. Prayer for Peace 166
4. Love Suffers Much 169
5. Joy Wasn't in Me 171
6. Enlarge Your Tent 172
7. Micah 174
8. Jerusalem 180
9. The Light Shines in the Darkness 183
10. Arise, Shine 186
11. John Nine 188
12. Many Gifts 192
13. Love Song 194
14. God's People 196
15. Communion Song 198
16. Benediction 200

Scripture Index 203
Hymn Index 208

Acknowledgments

This book grows out of ten years of directing weekly chapel for the Bethel College community and a lifetime of worshiping with the people of God in various church communities.

In planning chapels at Bethel from 1986-96, I worked with various student and faculty members of the Campus Ministries Team, whose support and creative participation enabled these efforts. Especially invaluable was the creative stewing and prayerful worrying of Dale Schrag, who was a member of the chapel planning committee for ten years.

A special word of thanks to two colleagues at Bethel who each collaborated with me on one of the pieces in this book. John McCabe-Juhnke (Associate Professor of Speech and Drama) worked with me on "A Thanksgiving Reading" and Raylene Hinz-Penner (former Associate Professor of English and now an Associate in the Development Office) did some important reflective brainstorming on "Ancient Advent Songs."

Although this collection has been a longtime personal dream, it was the nudging and nurture of Faith & Life Press that made this project a reality, especially Mark Regier (an alumnus of Bethel Campus Ministries Team) and Susan Janzen, who patiently shepherded me through the writing and publishing process.

The scripts and readings in this book are largely presentations of Scripture. In most cases, the text has been adapted from the Revised Standard Version and the author's own translation. Sometimes there have been modifications adapted from the New International Version or Today's English Version. In all cases, the intention has been to present a fresh and faithful proclamation of Scripture.

Except where noted, hymns suggested in this book can be found in *Hymnal: A Worship Book,* the hymnal of my denomination. Many of these hymns are familiar and can be found in other hymnals or songbooks. An index at the back of the book includes page numbers for songs in *Hymnal: A Worship Book.*

An Invitation

"Bless the Lord, O my soul, and all that is within me, bless God's holy name!" the psalmist sings (Psalm 103:1). This is not only the joyful response of an individual called to praise God, but also an invitation for the gathered congregation.

"Let all within us praise" is a plea to bring the full range of human emotion into our worship, but it is more. It is also a call to find a variety of ways to express and proclaim God's Word to us.

In response to that call, this book brings together forty-five readers theater scripts, all adapted from Scripture, and sixteen songs that I have developed and then used in settings ranging from spiritual retreats to congregational worship. Especially in the last ten years as I planned midweek worship for a college community, I have found myself turning again and again to dramatic reading and hymn singing as the preferred worship style of a lecture-weary campus congregation of students, faculty, and staff.

Each readers theater script is preceded by background information about the reading, notes for rehearsing it, and suggestions for worship planning. In some cases I suggest a theme for the whole service and include a call to worship, benediction, and hymn possibilities. You will, of course, need to adapt these ideas to fit your local situation.

In several instances I recommend that congregational members give brief reflections in place of a longer sermon. While I affirm the importance of the sermon, I am convinced that we must also find ways for members of the congregation to "give testimony" in our public worship. Occasionally inviting several people to give brief reflections on a common theme is one way to do this.

May these readings and songs call you to bless the Lord God of all creation in richer and fuller ways. Let all within you praise!

I

Using
Readers Theater
in Worship

Using Readers Theater in Worship

Hearing the Scripture read should be a high point of our worship together. Our Christian faith affirms that the Bible is the Word of God, spoken through generations and now proclaimed in ours. Through the guidance of the Holy Spirit, these words have been preserved for us because God intended them to be—and the people of God have found them to be—a living Word for evoking faith and nurturing spiritual growth. What a treasure for the church! We should be on the edge of our seats to hear this awesome Word proclaimed in our public gatherings!

Too often, Scripture reading in public worship is perfunctory. As worshipers, we often find it difficult to give attention to Scripture read aloud. We assume we already know what it says, so our minds wander.

This tendency to tune out the familiar is often compounded by the way Scripture is read. When reading the Bible in public, we sometimes adopt a tone of voice or style that I call "reading it as Scripture." This formal, stiff style intones the words with great respect for their holiness, but with little sense of their urgency and vibrancy. I regularly remind my student readers, "Please don't read it 'as Scripture.' Announce it as exciting news you can't wait to pass on to your friends!"

As a biblical scholar, I certainly affirm the need for careful Bible study. But as a pastor and worship leader, I also yearn for the Word to be proclaimed and heard in our worship. We need to experience the Scripture in both these ways to absorb its richness. How can we read Scripture in our worship so that it comes through as a contemporary word speaking to us? How can we challenge the congregation to sit up and give attention to God's Word?

Over the past fifteen years, I have used readers theater as one way to respond to these concerns. Readers theater can give added rhetorical force to Scripture by bringing together scriptural passages and repeating phrases and verses. Multiple readers encourage more attention and participation from an audience. In many worship services, I have seen this medium bring Scripture to life in a new way.

In creating these forty-five readings, I have adapted the words of Scripture for public proclamation, putting them in forms more pleasing to the ear. In doing this, I have taken care to be faithful to the scriptural intent. At the same time, I know that developing a readers theater script from Scripture involves interpretation. So worshipers will not blur the distinction between readers theater script and Holy Scriptures, whenever I list a readers theater piece in the order of service, I always add a line that says "adapted from" the biblical text.

How to Prepare for Readers Theater

Readers theater is not conventional drama; instead of memorizing lines and moving around a stage, people read from a script in a fairly fixed space. But neither is readers theater just reading.

It is dramatic reading involving oral interpretation of a text. While readers theater does not demand the long rehearsal time of much drama, it does require careful preparation to be effective.

The following step-by-step suggestions describe how to prepare a reading for use in public worship. If you are the pastor or worship planner but others will be rehearsing the readers theater piece, make sure they receive a copy of these instructions. And blessings on your preparation and worship!

Step 1: Choose your readers. You may want to recruit a group of people to perform the reading and give them copies of the script and the rehearsal notes for their reading. Also suggest that a "designated leader" read this "How to Prepare" section.

It also works for one person—either you or someone you invite—to be the director. The director coordinates the advance preparation and directs the rehearsal.

Readers theater offers a wonderful opportunity to broaden participation in leading worship. Sometimes you may choose all teenagers or young adults as your readers. Other times you may ask youth and adults to work together. Choose people who have public-speaking skills, but also consider inviting some whose gifts for drama and speaking may need encouragement and development.

Step 2: Set a time to rehearse. The readers' job is to make Scripture come alive in a fresh way for people who may have grown "tired" of hearing. This means they need to bring confidence and conviction to their presentation. These attitudes come only with practice. I have been able to adequately rehearse all but the longest scripts in one 45- to 60-minute session.

Step 3: Prepare the scripts. Make a copy of the script for each reader and highlight each reader's part with a marker. Put the scripts into identical folders. Small, hard-backed, three-ringed, black notebooks work well. They do not distract the audience during presentation, and they make scripts easier to hold and the turning of pages less conspicuous.

The director needs to read through the scripts before the rehearsal to become familiar with the intention of the reading, to note stage directions, and to highlight places that may require special practice.

Step 4: Hold the Rehearsal. The rehearsal is a time to prepare the readers and to prepare the reading for its presentation.

a. When you first gather, remind the readers (or each other) of the importance of your task. You have agreed not only to read Scripture, but also to proclaim it. Sometimes when Scripture is read in a worship service, people "tune out" because they think they've heard it before, or because it may not be read well. But your task is to make the Word of God come alive. In effect, you are preachers. You are proclaiming the Word of God! This is indeed important work!

b. Consider where the reading fits into the order of worship. This means you will need to look at the bulletin or talk to the pastor ahead of time. What is the theme of the service? What comes before and after the reading? If the reading is used as a call to worship, its tone will be exuberant and energetic; if it is used as a call to prayer, it may be quieter.

c. Read through the script together three or four times, stopping to work on the more complicated passages until they go smoothly. Review the rehearsal notes for your script and work through elements of staging. Don't hesitate to offer or ask for suggestions about how a particular line might be read more effectively. Consider which words or phrases in the script should be emphasized.

d. Think about how you as readers sound together. Many times a reader will have a complete sentence to read and can give expression to it in an individual way. Other times a sentence will be divided between several readers who must work together to express a complete thought. At those times, the readers have to cooperate in the cadence of their reading. Rather than pausing after each phrase, one reader must pick up immediately after the other so the sentence sounds like it is delivered by a single voice. To play a bit with Paul's analogy in 1 Corinthians 12, sometimes in readers theater, there are many bodies but one voice.

Sometimes several readers will read together, and they may be tempted to speak more softly or slowly. The point of multiple voices, however, is to increase the volume to add emphasis. In these places, encourage readers to read at their usual speed and volume. Rehearse these sections enough times that everyone feels comfortable with the inflection and flow of the lines.

Sometimes one voice will begin reading a sentence and other voices will join to create a crescendo as the sentence moves toward a climax. In this situation, the first reader should act as the leader, reading the sentence in a normal tone. The "added voices" are responsible to join in, matching the tone and rhythm of the first reader. Rehearse these sections until you can read them smoothly.

e. Decide where you will sit during the service. When you read, where will you stand and in what order? Usually readers stand in a line in front of the congregation, but in some situations readers may stand where they are seated in the congregation or speak from the balcony. Always consider how well you will be heard by people who may be hard of hearing. Use microphones if necessary.

Many readers theater groups open and close their books together. If you decide to do this, you will need to practice it ahead of time.

Hymn Singing and Scripture

Hymn singing and Scripture go together for me. Perhaps that is why I have often written folk hymns as a response to my work with biblical texts.

The hymns we sing express our theology and our faith. They invite us to interpret and savor the biblical word. Hymns are a wonderful vehicle to "let all within us praise!" They can be sung as preparation for hearing a particular reading, or as a response to a reading. As you use these readings, consider the ways music allows the congregation to participate in proclaiming and responding to the biblical message.

Many of the suggested hymns are widely used within the Christian church. Others are newer and may be more difficult to find. Often I suggest one of the songs I have written that appears at the back of this book. As a way of identifying at least one place where you can find each hymn, there is an index at the back of this book identifying the page number of hymns found in the two hymnal resources which I most often use: *Hymnal: A Worship Book* (Brethren Press, Faith & Life Press, and Mennonite Publishing House, 1992) and *Sing and Rejoice!* (Herald Press, 1979).

Finally, don't be intimidated by the prospect of coordinating readers theater, music, and the rest of your order of worship. Once you've tried it, you'll find that rehearsal is easier than it sounds. And it's well worth the effort to experience the joy of proclaiming the Word of God in a powerful new way for your congregation.

II

Dramatic Readings

With Heart, Soul, Mind, and Strength

1. With Thankful Hearts
2. With All Your Soul
3. Treasuring God's Wisdom
4. With All Your Strength
5. If You Do This, You Will Live

1. With Thankful Hearts

Background

The Great Commandment (Deuteronomy 6:5) begins with the call to love God "with all your heart." This reading presents the Deuteronomy text with an emphasis on thankful hearts. It reminds us that the wellspring of thanksgiving is an awareness that all we have is a gracious gift. Weaving together themes from Psalm 100 and Deuteronomy 6 and 8, the text calls us to gratitude and loyalty to God.

Rehearsal Notes

The script is designed for four readers. The opening and closing exhortation are the "envelope" into which the homily from Deuteronomy fits. Invite the readers to speak with enthusiasm, as if the congregation will be hearing these words for the first time.

At points in this reading, several readers read together. At these times, readers are often tempted to speak more softly or slowly; but the point of multiple voices is to increase volume and emphasis. Rehearse these sections until the readers feel comfortable with a common rhythm. When voices are added to a repeated line, the first reader should be the leader; the others should follow, matching the leader's cadence and tone.

The paragraph about the entry into the promised land contains several parenthetical comments. These should be read as sober reminders to the people to acknowledge God's provision in the midst of the excitement of these new possessions.

Worship Planning

I created this script and the others in this section for use in a series of four worship services where we considered the different aspects of the Great Commandment (as presented in Mark 12:28-34):

1. with all your heart;
2. with all your soul;
3. with all your mind;
4. with all your strength.

This reading was used in the first service and focused on loving God with grateful hearts. I wrote the song "Love the Lord (With All)" (No. 1 in this book) for that series.

This reading could also be used at a Thanksgiving service. Other hymns that could be used as a response to this reading:

"We Give Thanks unto You"

"Praise, I Will Praise You, Lord"

With Thankful Hearts

1	Let us give thanks to God with a whole heart
2	in the company of the whole congregation.
3	Give thanks to God!
4	Bless God's name!
2	God's love endures forever!

1,2,3,4	Hear, O Israel, the Lord our God, the Lord is one!
1	And you shall love the Lord your God with all your heart and soul and strength!
1,2	And you shall love the Lord your God with all your heart and soul and strength!
1,2,3,4	And you shall love the Lord your God with all your heart and soul and strength!
3	And these words shall be upon your heart,
4	and you shall teach them diligently to your children;
1	you shall talk of them when you sit in the house,
2	when you walk by the way,
3	when you lie down,
4	and when you rise....

1	And when the Lord your God brings you into the land
2	(that promised land, flowing with milk and honey)
3	with great cities,
2	(cities which you did not build),
4	and houses full of good things,
2	(houses which you did not fill),
3	and vineyards and olive trees,
2	(vineyards and trees which you did not plant)

1	and when you have eaten and taken your fill—
4	then take heed lest you forget the Lord;
2	(Give thanks to God with a whole heart)
4	lest you say in your heart,
3	"It is my power and my strength that have gotten me all this."
1	Remember that it is God who gives you the strength to achieve all these things!
2	(It is God who has made us, and not we ourselves.)

1   Let us give thanks to God with a whole heart

2   in the company of the whole congregation.

3   Give thanks to God!

4   Bless God's name!

1,2,3,4   God's love endures forever!

Adapted from Deuteronomy 6:4-7, 10-12; 8:17-18; Psalm 100:3-5; and Psalm 111:1.

2. With All Your Soul

Background

This reading invites us to reflect on the command to love God "with all your soul." The prayer in Ephesians 3:14-19 asks that God may strengthen our inner being (our souls) so we can grasp the full extent of God's love. The presentation of the Great Commandment here comes from Mark's account of Jesus' conversation with a scribe. The opening paragraph presents the Ephesians prayer as Paul's prayer for the church; the closing paragraph makes Paul's words our prayer to comprehend the love of God with all our soul.

Rehearsal Notes

This script is designed for four readers. They should stand in a line with Readers 2 and 3 on the ends; Readers 2 and 3 step forward during their scene. This will emphasize the dialogue between Jesus and the scribe.

At times in this reading, several persons read together. At these points they may be tempted to speak more softly or slowly; but the point of multiple voices is to increase volume and emphasis. Rehearse these sections until the readers feel comfortable with a common rhythm. When voices are added to a repeated line, the first reader should be the leader; the others should follow, matching the leader's cadence and tone.

Worship Planning

When this reading is used for a general presentation of Mark's text, either the song "Love the Lord (With All)" (No. 1 in this book) or the hymn "Be Thou My Vision" would make an appropriate response.

This script can also be used to develop the theme "with all your soul" in a four-part series on the Great Commandment. In such a context, I once used the following order of service. Note the frequent reference to "soul" in these hymns and texts:

Call to Worship	Psalm 103:1-5
Opening Hymn	"Praise, My Soul, the God of Heaven"
Responsive Reading	"Two Worlds of Experience" (46 in this book)
Readers Theater	"With All Your Soul"
Song	"Love the Lord (With All)"
Reflections	"Soul-searching and God-loving"
Prayer	
Closing Hymn	"When Peace, Like a River"

I've given you the title for the sermon (or reflections), but the substance is up to you!

With All Your Soul

1	For this reason, I bow my knees before God,
2	from whom every family in heaven and on earth is named,
3	that according to the riches of God's glory,
4	you may be strengthened in your inner being with power through the Spirit;
1	that Christ may dwell in your hearts through faith,
2	so that you are rooted and grounded in love,
3	(rooted and grounded in love);
4	that you may have the power to comprehend with all the saints,
2	what is the breadth and length and height and depth.

{Readers 2 and 3 step forward to accentuate dialogue.}

1	And one of the scribes, a teacher of Torah, came up to him and asked him,
2	"Which commandment is the greatest of all?"
1	Jesus answered,
3	"The first is:
1,3,4	Hear, O Israel, the Lord our God, the Lord is one!
3	And you shall love the Lord your God with all your heart,
3,4	with all your soul,
1,3,4	with all your mind,
1,2,3,4	and with all your strength.
3	The second is: Love your neighbor as yourself. If you do this, you will live.

1,2,3,4	If you do this, you will live.

1	And the scribe said,
2	"You are right, teacher, God is one. And to love God with all the heart and with all the understanding and with all the strength and to love one's neighbor as oneself is much more than all worship and praise."

3	"You have answered wisely—you are not far from the kingdom of God." *{Readers 2 and 3 step back into line.}*

1	Power to comprehend with all the saints,
4	what is the breadth and length and height and depth.
3	Love God with heart, soul, mind, and strength!
2	Love neighbor as yourself!
2,3	You are not far from the kingdom of God.
1	May Christ dwell in our hearts through faith,
2	so that we are rooted and grounded in love.
3	May we have the power to comprehend with all the saints
4	what is the breadth and length and height and depth.
1	May we know the love of Christ that surpasses knowledge,
2,3,4	and be filled with the fullness of God.

Adapted from Ephesians 3:14-19 and Mark 12:28-34.

3. Treasuring God's Wisdom

Background

What is the connection between loving God "with all your mind" and seeking God's wisdom? Jesus is often referred to in the New Testament as the wisdom of God (1 Corinthians 1:24; Colossians 2:3; Luke 11:49). This reading suggests a parallel between the figure of Lady Wisdom in Proverbs 1–2 and Jesus in the Gospels. We are invited to ponder two questions: What does it mean to love God with our mind? And what would it mean to see God's wisdom—and not earthly wealth—as the treasure worth pursuing?

Rehearsal Notes

The script is designed for four readers with minimal staging. At the beginning of the reading, Reader 3 is at the back of the room. The other three readers are standing in a line at the front. Reader 1 (scribe) and Reader 3 (who plays both Wisdom and Jesus), after reaching the front, should stand on opposite ends. This will emphasize the dialogue between them.

Twice, Reader 3 starts at the back of the room and walks down the aisle as noted in the script, portraying a figure moving through the busy streets of a city, while the other readers are speaking. This movement should be rehearsed, so that each time, Reader 3 arrives at the front just in time to read the appointed lines.

At times in this reading, several persons read together. At these points they may be tempted to speak more softly or slowly; but the point of multiple voices is to increase volume and emphasis. Rehearse these sections until the readers feel comfortable with a common rhythm. When voices are added to a repeated line, the first reader should be the leader; the others should follow, matching the leader's cadence and tone.

Worship Planning

This reading can be used in a service that explores the search for God's wisdom or the connection between faith and intellect.

It can also be used to develop the theme "with all your mind" in a four-part series on the Great Commandment. (See notes on Reading 1, "With Thankful Hearts.") As part of such a series, I once used the following order of service. Note the frequent references to the theme:

Call to Worship	Psalm 111:1-3, 10
Opening Hymn	"We Would Extol Thee"
Readers Theater	"Treasuring God's Wisdom"
Song	"Love the Lord (With All)" (No. 1 in this book)
Reflections/Sermon	
Prayer	
Hymn	"I Sought the Lord" or "Be Thou My Vision"
Benediction	Based on Ephesians 3:16-19

Treasuring God's Wisdom

1   Search for God's wisdom as for hidden treasure.

2   Treasure God with your heart and soul,
             with your mind and strength.

4   For where your treasure is, there will your life be.

        {Reader 3 walks up the aisle toward other readers.}

1   Look, there is wisdom!

4   She cries aloud in the open air!

2   She raises her voice in public places!

4   She calls in the middle of the busy street;

1   she preaches in the open gates of the city:

        {Reader 3 arrives at front, in time to begin speaking.}

3   "My children, my students, take my words to heart!
             And treasure up my commands in your mind.
             Give your heart to wisdom, your mind to understanding."

1   Yes, if you cry out for insight,

2   and raise your voice for understanding,

3   if you seek wisdom like silver—

4   and search for her like hidden treasure—

1   Then you will understand the fear of the Lord

2   and find the knowledge of God.

4   For the Lord bestows wisdom
             and teaches knowledge and understanding.

3   If you seek wisdom like silver—

1   and search for her like hidden treasure—

2   Then you will understand what is right and just,

4   what is fair and good, and what you should do.

3   For wisdom will sink into your mind,

4   and knowledge will be your heart's delight.

2   Discretion will watch over you

1   and understanding will guard you.

        {Reader 3 walks down aisle to the back of the room.}

1   Search for God's wisdom as for hidden treasure.

2   Treasure God with your heart and soul,
             with your mind and strength.

4   For where your treasure is, there will your life be!

{Reader 3 walks up aisle toward other readers.}

1	Look, there is Jesus!
4	He is walking in the temple courts,
2	he is teaching in the public square
4	and preaching in the midst of the people!

{Reader 3 arrives at the front to stand with other readers.}

2	And one of the scribes, a teacher of Torah, came up and asked him,
1	"Which commandment is the greatest of all?"
2	Jesus answered,
3	"The first is:
2,3,4	Hear, O Israel, the Lord our God, the Lord is one!
3	And you shall love the Lord your God with all your heart,
3,2	with all your soul,
3,2,4	with all your mind,
3,2,4,1	and with all your strength.
3	The second is: Love your neighbor as yourself. If you do this, you will live.
1,2,3,4	If you do this, you will live."

2	And the scribe said,
1	"You are right, teacher, God is one. And to love God with all the heart and with all the understanding and with all the strength and to love one's neighbor as oneself, is much more than all worship and praise."
2	And Jesus said,
3	"You have answered wisely— You are not far from the kingdom of God."

1	Search for God's wisdom as for hidden treasure.
2	Treasure God with your heart and soul, with your mind and strength.
4	For where your treasure is, there will your life be.
1,2,3,4	For where your treasure is,
3	there will your life be.

Adapted from Proverbs 1:20-21; 2:1-11; Mark 12:28-34; and Matthew 6:21.

4. With All Your Strength

Background

This is a straightforward presentation of themes in Deuteronomy 6, 8, and 10. The recurring phrase "do this with all your strength" emphasizes the completeness of God's claim on our lives and lifestyles. The closing part of the reading summarizes the prophetic message that God cares for the vulnerable in our society and expects justice from those who claim to love God.

Rehearsal Notes

This script is designed for four readers. At times in this reading, several persons read together. At these points they may be tempted to speak more softly or slowly; but the point of multiple voices is to increase volume and emphasis. Rehearse these sections until the readers feel comfortable with a common rhythm. When voices are added to a repeated line, the first reader should be the leader; the others should follow, matching the leader's cadence and tone until the reading climaxes with the final rendition by all four voices.

Worship Planning

This reading could be used in a service that focuses on the Deuteronomy passages in general.

It could also be used to develop the theme "with all your strength" in a four-part series on the Great Commandment. (See notes on Reading 1, "With Thankful Hearts.") As part of such a series, I once used the following order of service. Note the frequent references to the theme:

Call to Worship (from Psalm 84 and Isaiah 12 and 40)

Leader:	Blessed are those whose strength is in God, whose hearts are set on pilgrimage.
People:	*God does not faint or grow weary. God gives power to those who are exhausted, and to the weak, God increases strength.*
Leader:	They who wait upon the Lord shall renew their strength; they shall mount up with eagles' wings. They shall run and not be weary, they shall walk and not faint.
People:	*God is our strength and song! God has become our salvation!*

Opening Hymn	"God of Our Strength"
Readers Theater	"With All Your Strength"
Song	"Love the Lord (With All)" (No. 1 in this book)
Reflections/Sermon	
Prayer	
Hymn	"If All You Want, Lord"

Benediction (from Psalm 105, Isaiah 4, and Hebrews 12)

Leader:	Those who wait upon the Lord shall renew their strength. Look to the Lord and seek God's strength continually.
People:	*We will seek to love God with heart and soul and mind and strength!*
Leader:	Lift your drooping hands and strengthen your weak knees; make straight paths for your feet!
People:	*Let us run with perseverance the race that is set before us, looking to Jesus, the pioneer and perfecter of our faith.*

Response	"Guide My Feet"

With All Your Strength

1	Now these are the commandments, which the Lord, your God, commanded me to teach you, that you may do them in the land into which you are going.
2	That you might fear the Lord, your God, by keeping all God's commandments, all the days of your life,
3	you and your children and your children's children, that your life may be prolonged—
4	Do this with all your strength!
1,2,3,4	Hear, O Israel, the Lord our God, the Lord is one!
1	And you shall love the Lord your God with all your heart and soul and strength.
1,2	And you shall love the Lord your God with all your heart and soul and strength.
1,2,3,4	And you shall love the Lord your God with all your heart and soul and strength!
3	And these words shall be upon your heart, and you shall teach them diligently to your children.
2	You shall talk of them when you sit in the house,
1	when you walk by the way,
4	when you lie down, when you rise.
3	Do this with all your strength.
1	And when the Lord your God brings you into the land, which God swore to your ancestors to give you—
2	with great and goodly cities
4	(which you did not build),
3	and houses full of all good things
4	(which you did not fill),
1	and cisterns dug out
4	(which you did not dig),
2	and vineyards and olive trees
4	(which you did not plant),
3	and when you eat and are full—
4	then take heed, lest you forget the Lord;
1,2	take heed lest you forget the Lord.

3   Beware, lest you say in your heart,
"My power and the strength of my hand have gotten me this wealth."

4   You shall remember the Lord your God,
for it is God who gives you the strength to get wealth.

1   (Love the Lord with all your strength!)

2   And now, Israel, what does the Lord require of you?

1   To fear God, love God, walk in all God's ways,

3   to serve the Lord your God with all your heart and soul and
strength.

4   For the Lord your God is God of gods and Lord of lords,

2   who executes justice for the orphan and widow,

3   who loves the sojourner, giving them food and clothing.

1   Therefore, love the sojourner in your midst,

4   for you were sojourners in the land of Egypt.

1   You shall love the Lord your God
with all your heart and soul and strength.

1,2   You shall love the Lord your God
with all your heart and soul and strength.

1,2,3,4   You shall love the Lord your God
with all your heart and soul and strength!

2   Do this with all your strength.

Adapted from Deuteronomy 6:1-12; 8:17-18; and 10:12, 17-19.

5. If You Do This, You Will Live

Background

After eliciting the Great Commandment from a lawyer, Jesus says, "If you do this, you will live" (Luke 10:25-28). As a reflection on Jesus' call to *live* this commandment, this script presents two teaching scenes from Jesus' life. The first is the account of a widow who gives all she has, though meager it may seem. The second story is the dramatic parable of the sheep and goats. Both illustrate the value Jesus placed on living out our claims to love God.

Rehearsal Notes

This script is designed for four readers. At times in this reading, several persons read together. At these points they may be tempted to speak more softly or slowly; but the point of multiple voices is to increase volume and emphasis. Rehearse these sections until the readers feel comfortable with a common rhythm. When voices are added to a repeated line, the first reader should be the leader; the others should follow, matching the leader's cadence and tone until the reading climaxes with the final rendition by all four voices.

Feel free to use dramatic gestures with this script. For example, readers could act out the "large sums" and the "two copper coins" being dropped into the offering. And in the parable of the sheep and goats, "Jesus" could motion the "sheep" and "goats" to appropriate sides when he addresses them.

Worship Planning

This reading can be used in a service that focuses on living out the Great Commandment.

It can also be used to develop the theme "with all your strength" in a four-part series on the Great Commandment. (See notes on Reading 1, "With Thankful Hearts.") Used in this way, it would be an alternative to the previous reading. See the worship planning comments for that script. The hymn "I Bind My Heart This Tide" reenforces the themes of this reading nicely.

If You Do This, You Will Live

1	A lawyer stood up to put Jesus to the test,
2	"Teacher, what shall I do to inherit eternal life?"
3	"What is written in the law? How do you read?"
2	"You shall love the Lord your God with all your heart, and with all your soul, and with all your mind, and with all your strength; and your neighbor as yourself."
3	"You have answered right. If you do this, you will live."
4	(If you do this, you will live).
1	Jesus sat down opposite the treasury in the temple, watching the multitude putting money into the offering.
3	Some people put in large sums.
4	A poor widow came and put in two copper coins that make a penny.
1	And Jesus called his disciples and said to them,
2	"Truly I say to you, this poor widow has put in more than all the others who have given offerings. For they all contributed a little out of their abundance, but she has given her whole living, all that she has."
1	"You shall love the Lord your God with all your heart,
1,2	and with all your soul,
1,2,3	and with all your mind,
1,2,3,4	and with all your strength;
2	and your neighbor as yourself.
3	If you do this, you shall live.
1,2,3,4	If you do this, you shall live.
3	When the Son of Man comes in his glory and all the angels with him, he will sit on his glorious throne. Before him will be gathered all the nations.
1	And he will separate them one from another as a shepherd separates the sheep from the goats.
2	He will place the sheep at his right hand, but the goats at his left.
3	Then the king will say to those at his right hand,
4	"Come, O blessed of my Father, inherit the kingdom prepared for you.

> For I was hungry and you gave me food.
> I was thirsty and you gave me drink,
> I was a stranger and you welcomed me,
> I was naked and you clothed me,
> I was sick and you visited me,
> I was imprisoned and you came to me!"

1   "Lord, when did we see you hungry and feed you,
      or thirsty and give you drink?
      When did we see you a stranger or naked or sick
      or imprisoned and minister to you?"

4   "Truly I say to you, as you did it to one of the least of these,
      you did it to me."
      "Depart from me, you cursed, into the eternal fire!
      For I was hungry and thirsty and you gave me nothing!
      I was a stranger and naked and you did not care for me!
      I was sick and in prison and you did not come to me!"

2   "Lord, when did we see you in such situations
      and did not minister to you? When?"

4   "Truly I say to you, as you did it NOT to one of the least of
      these, you did it not to me."

1   "You shall love the Lord your God with all your heart,

1,2   and with all your soul,

1,2,3   and with all your mind,

1,2,3,4   and with all your strength;

2   and your neighbor as yourself.

3   If you do this, you shall live.

1,2,3,4   If you do this, you shall live.

Adapted from Luke 10:25-28; Matthew 25:31-46; and Mark 12:41-44.

Let All Within You Praise

6. A Modern Psalm: Call to Praise

7. Bless the Lord, O My Soul

8. Know and Serve the Lord with Gladness

9. Declare God's Marvelous Works

10. God Is Our Refuge and Strength

11. How Can We Sing in a Strange New Land?

12. Lord, You Have Searched Me

13. Two Worlds of Experience

14. A Cry from the Depths

15. Through the Valley of the Shadow

16. Responsive Reading on Psalm 23 and the Beatitudes

6. A Modern Psalm: Call to Praise

Background

The psalms often called the people to praise God by invoking the beauty and wonder of the Creator's world. This contemporary psalm extends the invitation to praise by drawing aspects of our modern world into the orbit of God's sovereignty. Many psalms are echoed here, but Psalms 19, 96, 148, and 150 are most obvious.

Rehearsal Notes

This script is for two readers. As they are, in effect, "town criers" calling creation and congregation to praise God, they should speak with enthusiasm.

The readers should rehearse the unison lines until they are comfortable with each other's rhythm and timing. The point of such unison reading is to increase the volume and emphasis of the lines.

Feel free to update the psalm even more by adapting it to fit your specific circumstances. The nouns in the closing lines of the reading may be changed to include aspects of your immediate worship setting, such as "with choirs and Bible school" or "with picnics and pageants."

Worship Planning

This reading makes an excellent call to worship. Follow it with a hymn that picks up the theme of all creation praising God:

"Let the Whole Creation Cry"

"All Creatures of Our God and King"

"Earth and All Stars"

This last hymn picks up the call of "engines and steel" to join all creation in praising God.

A Modern Psalm: A Call to Praise

1,2	God is creating the heavens and the earth
1	and the heavens are telling the glory of God.
2	Oh come, let us sing to the Lord!
1,2	Let all that has life and breath, sing to the glory of God!
1	Sing to the Lord, all the earth!
2	Let the heavens be glad, let the sea roar,
1	let the cities exult, let the boulevards sing for joy!
1,2	Praise the Lord, all creation!
1	Sing, sun and moon!
2	Sing, all you shining factories!
1,2	Praise the Lord, all creation!
2	Mountains and hills, Fords and Hondas!
1	Beasts and all cattle, shopping malls and restaurants!
1,2	Praise the Lord, all creation!
1	Leaders and peoples, young and old,
2	women, and men, and children together!
1,2	Praise the Lord, all creation!
1	With worship and work!
2	With teaching and learning!
1	With drama and singing!
2	With laughter and talking!
1,2	Praise the Lord, all creation!
1	Oh come, let us sing to the Lord!
2	Let all that has life and breath
1,2	sing to the glory of God!

Adapted from Psalm 19:1; Psalm 96:1, 11-12; Psalm 148:3, 9-12; and Psalm 150:6.

7. Bless the Lord, O My Soul

Background

Our faith journey is one of constant growth and transformation, surrounded by the sure provisions of God. This reading incorporates passages from Psalm 103, Ephesians 4, and Romans 12 that remind us of "all God's benefits" in the midst of a call to "be transformed by the renewal of our minds" and to "grow up into Christ." I wrote this script for a worship service whose theme was "The Growing Edge of Faith."

Rehearsal Notes

This script is for four readers. At one point, several persons read together. While readers may be tempted to speak more softly or slowly, the point here is to increase volume and even tempo somewhat. Rehearse this section until all feel comfortable with a common rhythm.

In another place, one reader begins a sentence and other voices join in. In this case, the first reader acts as leader, reading the whole phrase at a comfortable pace. The others join in, matching the cadence of the phrase until the climax, "and upbuilds itself in love."

Worship Planning

This reading can be used as a call to worship, followed by "Praise, My Soul, the King of Heaven," a hymn which is based on Psalm 103.

I once used the following opening to a worship service which included this reading:

Choral Invocation	"Holy, Holy, Holy," sung by choir or ensemble
Opening Prayer	
Leader:	Holy God of Hosts, the whole earth is full of your glory!
People:	*O God, we come into your presence as those who need the renewing touch of your Spirit to center our busy lives, to calm our frantic hearts, to heal our wounded souls. (time of silence)*
Leader:	Create in us clean hearts, O God, and renew a right spirit within us.
People:	*Restore to us the joy of your salvation and uphold us with your Spirit.*
Opening Hymn	"Create My Soul Anew"
Readers Theater	"Bless the Lord, O My Soul"
Hymn of Praise	"When All Thy Mercies, O My God"
Prayer	

Bless The Lord, O My Soul

1	Bless the Lord, O my soul, and all that is within me, bless God's holy name.
2	Bless the Lord, O my soul, and forget not all God's benefits,
1	who forgives all your sin,
3	who heals all your diseases,
4	who redeems your life from the Pit,
1	who crowns you with steadfast love and mercy,
2	who satisfies you with good as long as you live so that your youth is renewed like the eagle's.
3	Brothers and sisters, by the mercies of God, present your bodies as a living sacrifice,
4	holy and acceptable to God, "the worship offered by mind and heart."[1]
3	Be not *conformed* to this world,
4	but be *transformed* by the renewal of your mind,
3	that you may prove what is the will of God, what is good, acceptable, and perfect.
1	"Don't let the world around you squeeze you into its own mold,
2	but let God remold your minds from within, so that you may prove in practice
1	that God's plan for you is good ... and moves toward the goal of maturity."[2]
4	No longer will you be children tossed to and fro,
3	carried about with every wind of doctrine by human cunning,
2	by craftiness and deceitful wiles.
4	Rather, speaking the truth in love, you will grow up in every way into Christ,
3	(grow up into Christ)
1	from whom the whole body, joined and knit together by every joint with which it is supplied,
1,2	when each part is working properly,
1,2,3	makes bodily growth
1,2,3,4	and upbuilds itself in love.
4	Grow up in every way into Christ.
2	Be transformed by the renewal of your mind.

1	Bless the Lord, O my soul, and all that is within me, bless God's holy name.
2	Bless the Lord, O my soul, and forget not all God's benefits,
1	who forgives all your sin,
3	who heals all your diseases,
4	who redeems your life from the Pit,
1	who crowns you with steadfast love and mercy,
2	who satisfies you with good as long as you live so that your youth is renewed like the eagle's.
4	Bless the Lord, O my soul, and ALL that is within me, bless God's holy name.

[1]New English Bible. Oxford: Oxford University Press, 1970.
[2]The New Testament in Modern English, translated by J. B. Phillips. New York: Macmillan, 1958.

Adapted from Psalm 103:1-5; Ephesians 4:14-16; and Romans 12:1-2.

8. Know and Serve the Lord with Gladness

Background

This script is an interpretation of Psalm 100, but it takes as its theme verse 1 Chronicles 28:9: "Know and serve God with a whole heart and a willing mind." Deuteronomy 6:10-12 reflects on what it means to know that God is God and Romans 12 explores what it means to serve God. Undergirding it all is a sense of joy, for we do both "with gladness."

Rehearsal Notes

This script is for two readers. The paragraph from Deuteronomy contains a number of parenthetical comments, which almost suggest an internal dialogue. These should be read as a sober reminder to the listener to acknowledge God's provision, in the midst of the exciting gifts we receive, which we may think we have earned.

Worship Planning

Consider the following order of service:

Call to Worship	Psalm 100
Opening Hymn	"Joyful, Joyful, We Adore Thee"
Readers Theater	"Know and Serve God"
Call to Prayer	
Leader:	Know and serve God with a whole heart and with a willing mind; for the Lord searches all hearts and understands every plan and thought.
People:	*Search us, O God, and know our hearts. Probe us and know our thoughts. Lead us in the way everlasting.*
Silent Reflection and Prayer	
Prayer Hymn	"I Sought the Lord" or "Teach Me Thy Truth"

Know and Serve the Lord with Gladness

1	Make a joyful noise to the Lord, all peoples!
2	Serve God with gladness—rejoice!
1	Enter these gates with thanksgiving and praise!
2	Serve God with gladness—rejoice!

1	Know that the Lord is God! It is God who has made us and not we ourselves.
2	We are God's people, the sheep of God's pasture. Know and serve God with gladness.

1	Know and serve God with a whole heart and a willing mind.
2	For the Lord searches all hearts and understands every plan and thought.
1	If you search for God, you will find God.
2	Know and serve God with gladness!

1	And when God brings you into the land—
2	(that promised land, flowing with milk and honey)
1	with great cities
2	(cities which you did not build),
1	and houses full of good things
2	(houses which you did not fill),
1	and vineyards and olive trees
2	(vineyards and trees which you did not plant),
1	and when you have eaten and taken your fill— then take heed lest you forget the Lord,
2	(know and serve God!)
1	lest you say in your heart,
2	"It is my power and my strength that have gotten me all this."
1	Know that the Lord is God.
2	It is God who has made us and not we ourselves.
1	Know and serve God with gladness.

1,2	Therefore, brothers and sisters,
2	because of God's great mercies, offer your very selves to the Lord as a living sacrifice,
1	dedicated to God's service, fit for divine acceptance, "the worship offered by mind and heart."[3]

2	Do not be conformed to this world,
1	but be transformed by the renewal of your mind
2	that you may prove what is the will of God,
1	what is good and acceptable and perfect.
2	Know and serve God with a whole heart and a willing mind.
1	For the Lord searches all hearts and understands every plan and thought.
1,2	Know and serve God with gladness.

[3]New English Bible. Oxford: Oxford University Press, 1970.

Adapted from Psalm 100; 1 Chronicles 28:9; Deuteronomy 6:10-12; 8:17-18; and Romans 12:1-2.

9. Declare God's Marvelous Works

Background

The call to "declare God's marvelous works" echoes from the Psalms to the New Testament. Psalm 145 declares that we are to give such testimony—from generation to generation and to all peoples. The passage in 1 Peter 2 also claims that the purpose of our peoplehood is to "declare God's wonderful deeds." Finally, Paul exhorts that although what we preach is "a treasure in earthen vessels," it is Christ who is made visible.

Rehearsal Notes

This script is designed for three readers. At several points, all three readers speak together to add volume and emphasis to those phrases. Rehearse these sections until all readers are comfortable with the cadence of these phrases. Encourage the readers to read with enthusiasm, proclaiming the Scripture as if the congregation is hearing these words for the first time. As readers, you yourselves are giving testimony!

Worship Planning

This reading could be preceded by Psalm 96 as a call to worship and "Oh, That I Had a Thousand Voices" as an opening hymn. "Praise, I Will Praise You, Lord" can follow the reading, or a choir or ensemble can sing "God's People" (No. 14 in this book).

Declare God's Marvelous Works

1	Great is the Lord and greatly to be praised,
2	God's greatness is unsearchable.
3	One generation shall laud your works to another, and declare your mighty acts.
2	On the glorious splendor of your majesty, and on your wonderful works, we will meditate.
1,2,3	Great is the Lord and greatly to be praised!
3	O God, all your works shall give thanks to you, and all your saints shall bless you.
1	They shall speak of your glory,
2	they shall tell of your power,
1,2,3	they shall declare your marvelous works to all people!
3	Come to the Lord, to that Living Stone, rejected by the world, but chosen by God.
2	Come to that Living Stone,
1	and be yourselves like living stones, built into a spiritual house to the glory of God.
2	For you are a chosen race,
1	a royal priesthood,
3	a holy nation,
2	God's own people,
1	that you may declare the wonderful deeds of God who has called you out of darkness into marvelous light!
3	Once you were no people,
2	now you are God's people.
1	Once "you had no experience of mercy,
2	now it is intimately yours!"[4]
1,2,3	Great is the Lord and greatly to be praised.
1	For what we preach is not ourselves, but Jesus Christ as Lord,
2	with ourselves as your servants for Jesus' sake.
3	For it is the God who said, "Let light shine out of darkness," who has shone in our hearts
2	to give the light of the knowledge of the glory of God in the face of Christ.

1	We have this treasure in earthen vessels,
3	to show that the transcendent power belongs to God and not to us.
2	We are afflicted in every way, but not crushed;
3	perplexed, but not driven to despair;
1	persecuted, but not forsaken;
2	struck down, but not destroyed;
3	always carrying in the body the death of Jesus,
2	so that the life of Jesus may also be made visible in our bodies.
1	Great is the Lord and greatly to be praised!
2	Speak of God's glory,
3	tell of God's power,
1,2,3	declare God's marvelous works among all people!

⁴New English Bible. Oxford: Oxford University Press, 1970.

Adapted from Psalm 145:3-5, 10-12; 1 Peter 2:4-5, 9-10, and 2 Corinthians 4:5-10.

10. God Is Our Refuge and Strength

Background

This reading is a juxtaposition of Psalm 146 with Psalm 46. Its focus is on the presence and character of God as the source of our strength and confidence. While Psalm 46 uses natural metaphors (earthquake and storm) to describe the forces that threaten us, the script makes clear connections to the stresses and uncertainty of our everyday lives.

Rehearsal Notes

This script is for four readers. The repetition in the reading is intended to assure people of God's pervasive strength and to invite them to center themselves in the stillness of the divine presence.

The opening and closing parts of the reading are more reflective, while the middle section (Psalm 146) should be presented more enthusiastically, with the tempo and pitch increasing until it climaxes in the line "but the way of the wicked...." The section "Be still ..." should be a clear contrast to what precedes it—read in subdued tones with deliberate pauses, as one invites listeners to "be still and know...."

Worship Planning

This reading can be used in many ways, either as the opening declaration in a worship service, followed by a hymn like "God of Our Strength" or "Great is Thy Faithfulness"; or as a call to prayer, followed by a chorus like "They That Wait Upon the Lord." If used as a call to prayer, it would be appropriate to spend some time in silence, since the psalm calls us to "be still."

God Is Our Refuge and Strength

1	God is.
2	God is.
3	God is our refuge.
4	God is our refuge and strength.
3	A very present help.
4	A very present help in time of trouble.
1,2,3,4	God is our refuge and strength.

2	Therefore we will not fear though the earth should change,
1	though the mountains shake in the heart of the sea.
3	Therefore we will not fear though our lives should change,
4	though our hearts shake with questions and doubts.
2	The Lord of hosts is with us
4	The God of Jacob and Rachel is our refuge.
1	God is.
2	God is our refuge.
3	God is our refuge and strength.

4	"Let us never forget that this world and everything in it belong to God."[5]
1	Happy is the one whose hope is in the Lord God!
2	Who made heaven and earth!
3	Who keeps faith forever!

4	Who works justice for the oppressed!
3	Who gives food to the hungry!
2	The Lord sets the prisoners free!
1	The Lord opens the eyes of the blind!
2	The Lord loves the righteous,
1	and watches over the sojourners,
3	and upholds the widow and fatherless,
2	but the way of the wicked, God brings to ruin!
4	Let us never forget that this world and everything in it belong to God.

1	Be still.
2	Be still and know.
3	Be still and know that God is God.
1	Be still.
2	Be still and know.
3	Be still and know that God is God.
1	God is.
2	God is.
3	God is our refuge.
4	God is our refuge and strength.
3	A very present help.
4	A very present help in time of trouble.
1,2,3,4	God is our refuge and strength.

[5]From Psalm 24 in *Psalms Now* by Leslie Brandt. St. Louis: Concordia Publishing, 1973, p. 39.

Adapted from Psalm 46:1-3, 10-11 and Psalm 146:5-9.

11. How Can We Sing in a Strange New Land?

Background

This script presents a dialogue between parts of Psalm 137 and parts of Psalm 90. The first is a voice of lament, asking in a tragic time, "How can we sing?" The second is a voice of gratitude in a prosperous time, celebrating, "How can we keep from singing?" The ongoing dialogue is interrupted by the prophetic promise of God's coming (Isaiah 58:8-10). God is the one who announces in every time and place, "Here I am!" Confidence in God's constant presence both in our lament and our thanksgiving is the source of faithful song.

Rehearsal Notes

This script is for four readers. Encourage readers to present the emotional contrast between lament (Readers 1 and 2) and gratitude (Readers 3 and 4) in the manner and tone of their reading.

The final section (beginning with "Then shall your light …") should build in tempo and volume. The climax for this section comes with the line "God of the song…." The two readers who say "Here I am" are announcing God's presence; they should speak together with confidence and authority. Rehearse this section until all readers feel a comfortable crescendo and cadence.

The last five lines are a reprise of the whole dialogue, and the final "Here I am!" should be a resounding reminder of God's presence.

Worship Planning

The metaphor of this reading is the journey of faith as singing or song. Your worship service should include elements that give voice to both lament and gratitude, undergirded with the melody of trust in God. Consider or adapt the following order:

A Psalm of Trust (from Isaiah 62 and Isaiah 12)

Leader:	For God alone my soul waits in silence; from the Lord comes my salvation.
People:	*God alone is my rock and my salvation, my fortress; I shall never be shaken.*
Leader:	Trust in God at all times, O people! Pour out your heart before the Lord. God is a refuge for us.
People:	*Behold, God is our salvation; we will trust and not be afraid, for the Lord is our strength and our song.*

Hymn   "If You But Trust in God"

Psalms of Lament and Gratitude   "How Can We Sing in a Strange New Land?"

Reflections

Hymn   "My Life Flows On"

Closing Word of Trust (Habakkuk 3:17-18)

Leader:	Though the fig tree does not blossom, and no fruit is on the vines,
People:	*Though the fields yield no food, and the flock is cut off from the fold,*
Leader:	Yet we will rejoice in the Lord; we will exalt in the God of our salvation.
People:	*The Lord is our strength and our song; God has become our salvation.*

How Can We Sing in a Strange New Land?

1	By the waters of Babylon, we sat down and wept.
2	On the trees we hung up our harps when we remembered Jerusalem.
1	For there the people said, "Sing!
2	Sing!
1	Sing us one of the songs of Zion!"
2	How can we sing?
1	Can we sing to the Lord?
2	How can we sing in this strange new land?
1	In this strange new land, we hung up our harps.
2	"Sing!
1	Sing!
2	Sing us one of the old songs!"
1	How can we sing?
2	Can we sing to the Lord?
1	How can we sing in this strange new land?
3	O Lord, you have been our dwelling place in all generations.
4	Before the world was created, before we were born—
3	from everlasting to everlasting, you are God.
4	O Lord, you have been our home in all generations!
3	How can we keep from singing?
4	Satisfy us in the morning with your love that we may sing praises all our days.
3	O Lord, you have been our home in this generation—
4	How can we keep from singing?
1	By the waters of this strange land,
2	we sat down in despair—
1	we gave up our singing, when we thought of our home!
2	How can we sing?
1	Can we sing to the Lord?
2	How can we sing in this strange new land?

3	Then shall your light break forth like the morning.
4	Your night will become as the noonday sun.
3	You will call to the Lord,
4	and the Lord will answer.
3	You will cry, and God will say,
3,4	"HERE I AM!"
1	Your dwelling place in this generation!
3,4	HERE I AM!
2	Your home in this strange new land!
3,4	HERE I AM!
1	Your God—your refuge and strength!
3,4	HERE I AM!
2	God of the song and the strange new land!
1	How shall we sing in this strange new land?
3	Lord, you have been our dwelling place in all generations!
2	How shall we sing in this strange new land?
4	How can we keep from singing?
1,2,3,4	HERE I AM!

Adapted from Psalms 137:1-4; 90:1-2, 14; and Isaiah 58:8-10.

12. Lord, You Have Searched Me

Background

As Jacob was leaving Bethel, the morning after his dream and his new awareness that "the Lord was in this place and I did not know it" (Genesis 28:10-19), he could easily have spoken the words of Psalm 139. This reading juxtaposes portions of these two texts and invites the listener to consider how God is with us in all of life's circumstances.

Rehearsal Notes

The script is for four readers. It can be read straightforwardly or dramatized as follows. "Jacob" (Reader 4) can pantomime the first part of the script, walking down the aisle as he journeys toward Bethel, arriving at a spot where he "sleeps" before he awakes to speak. You will have to rehearse the timing of these movements to correspond to the reading of the script.

Worship Planning

This reading might be used as a call to prayer after an initial time of praise. Consider the possible sequence:

Time of Prayer	
Congregational Prayer	"Lead Me, Lord"
Scripture Reading	"Lord, You Have Searched Me"
Congregational Prayer	"Lead Me, Lord"
Time of Silence	
Pastoral Prayer	

The short refrain, "Lead Me, Lord," serves as an introduction and response to the readers theater piece. An accompanist can call the congregation to prayer by playing through the refrain each time, so that no verbal introduction is necessary.

Lord, You Have Searched Me

1	Lord, you have searched me and known me!
2	You have traced my journey and my resting places.
3	You are familiar with all my ways.
2	Lord, you have searched me and known me!

1	Jacob left Beersheba, and began his journey.
3	He came to a certain place, and stayed there that night because the sun had set.
1	Taking one of the stones on the ground, he put it under his head, and laid down to sleep.
3	And he dreamed that there was a ladder set upon the earth and the top of it reached to the heavens.
1	The angels of God were ascending and descending upon it.
3	And God stood above it and said,
2	"I am Yahweh, the God of Abraham and Sarah, the God of your father and mother ... I will give this land to you and your descendants. By you and your descendants, all the families of the earth shall bless themselves. Behold, I am with you and will keep you wherever you go. I will not leave you until I have done what I promised."

1	And Jacob awoke from his sleep and said,
4	"Surely God is in this place, and I did not know it! This is none other than the house of God! This is the gate of heaven."
3	And he called that place Bethel,
2	(that is, "House of God").

1	Lord, you have searched me and known me!
2	You know if I am standing or sitting,
3	you perceive my thoughts from afar.
4	You have traced my journey and my resting places.
1	You are familiar with all my ways.
2	Lord, you have searched me and known me!
3	Before a word is on my tongue, you know it completely.
4	Close behind and close in front—you surround me,
1	sheltering me with your hand.
2	Such knowledge is beyond my understanding,
3	unsearchable, beyond my reach.

1   Where can I go to escape your Spirit?

2   What if I would try to flee from your presence?

3   If I climb to the heavens, you are there.

4   If I sink to the depths, you are there too!

1   If I fly to the point of the sunrise—

2   or far across the sea—

3   your hand would still be guiding me,

4   your right hand holding me.

1   If I asked darkness to cover me:

2   ("Let there be night instead of light!")

3   Even darkness is not dark to you.

4   Night would shine as day for you.

1   Such knowledge is too wonderful,

4   unsearchable, beyond my reach.

1   Search me, O God, and know my heart.

2   Test me and know my thoughts.

3   See if there is any wicked or hurtful way in me.

4   And lead me in the way everlasting.

1   Search me, O God, and know my heart.

2   Test me and know my thoughts.

3   See if there is any wicked or hurtful way in me.

4   And lead me in the way everlasting.

Adapted from Psalm 139:1-12, 23-24 and Genesis 28:10-19.

13. Two Worlds of Experience

Background

While the Psalmist seems very comfortable lamenting before God, our modern worship rarely invites the worshiper to acknowledge struggle and despair. The following reading juxtaposes two psalms which express different aspects of the life of faith: Psalm 23 is an expression of trusting confidence, while Psalm 42 is the anguished cry of a soul responding to the silence of God.

Rehearsal Notes

This reading may be done by two readers, responsively, thus representing the two different voices from the Psalms. But it is better used as a responsive reading by the congregation. Be sure to give an introduction, adapted from the suggestions below, so the congregation is clear and comfortable with how they are invited to participate.

Worship Planning

This reading allows the expression of both lament and praise in a worship service. Print the text in the bulletin and use it as a responsive reading. Adapt the following introduction to your context, being sure to put the congregation at ease about how they are to participate, and being as clear and concise as you can about the instructions.

Introduction:

I invite you to participate in the reading on two worlds of experience as printed in your bulletin. This reading places two psalms side by side. The indented lines from Psalm 23 express the voice of confidence and trust in God's presence. The other lines from Psalm 42 describe the struggle and lament of the psalmist.

When we read this psalm responsively in a moment, I invite you to read the psalm that best expresses the state of your spirit this morning. Think about the week you have just lived through: What has it been like? Has your heart been full of joyful trust like Psalm 23 or heavy with thirsting and struggle like Psalm 42? Have you been more aware of God's presence or God's distance in your days?

If you identify more with the questions of the psalmist searching for God, then read the lines printed along the margin. If you identify more with the quiet confidence of Psalm 23, read the indented lines.

Let us come before God from whatever world of experience we are living through. Let us read responsively.

This reading can then be followed by a pastoral prayer or a prayer hymn. Some suggestions:
"From the Depths of Sin"
"I Sought the Lord"
"O Love That Will Not Let Me Go"

Two Worlds of Experience
(From Psalm 42 and Psalm 23)

As a hart pants for flowing streams, so longs my soul for you,
O God. My soul thirsts for God, for the Living God.

> The Lord is my shepherd, I shall not want.
> The Lord makes me lie down in green pastures.

When shall I come and behold the face of God? My tears have been my
food day and night, while people say to me, "Where is your God?"

> The Lord leads me beside still waters and restores
> my soul. The Lord leads me in paths of righteousness
> for the sake of God's name.

My soul is downcast within me. I say to God, my Rock,
"Why have you forgotten me?"

> Even though I walk through the valley
> of the shadow of death, I fear no evil,
> for thou art with me. Thy rod and thy staff
> comfort me.

Why are you cast down, O my soul, and why are you disquieted
within me?

> Surely goodness and mercy shall follow me all the
> days of my life and I shall dwell in the house
> of the Lord forever.

14. A Cry from the Depths

Background

This reading gives full expression to the voice of lament and expectation by combining Psalm 130 and Psalm 62. Too often our worship fails to acknowledge this dimension of experience, although the Psalms testify to its power in the life of the person of faith. After all, how can we give thanks to God for deliverance, if we are hesitant to confess before God the despairing and empty state of our souls? The purpose of this reading is to make a place in our worship for acknowledging the struggle that is an essential part of the dynamic rhythm of faith.

Rehearsal Notes

This script is for four readers. Ask the readers to identify the different moods that occur in the text, to note the dynamic of lament and quiet trust in the reading and then to express that in their tone. Their task is to invite the congregation to identify with the psalmist's message by the way they read. Invite them to read the psalm as a contemporary word of hope for a struggling community.

Worship Planning

In worship planning, I often follow an opening section of praise with a more reflective prayer or lament, thus embodying the range of expression we often find in the Psalms. I have often used this reading this way, as the following order of service suggests. Adapt it for your context.

> Call to Worship (from Psalm 103:1-5)
> Hymn of Praise   "Praise, My Soul, the King of Heaven!"
> A Call to Prayer and Reflection "A Cry from the Depths"
> Hymn of Prayer   "From the Depths of Sin"

I have written two songs that could also be used as a response to this reading: "Joy Wasn't in Me" (No. 5 in this book) traces the movement from lament to praise; "Love Suffers Much" (No. 4 in this book) explores the mystery of human suffering and God's response to it.

A Cry from the Depths

1	For God alone my soul waits in silence;
2	from God comes my salvation.
3	The Lord is my rock and my salvation,
4	my fortress; I shall never be shaken.
1	How long will you attack a person,
2	will you batter your victim, all of you,
1	as you would a tottering wall, a sagging fence?
3	Their only plan is to destroy,
4	They take pleasure in falsehood;
3	With their mouths they utter blessing,
4	but in their hearts they curse.
1	For God alone my soul waits in silence,
2	my hope is in God.
3	God alone is my rock and my salvation,
4	my fortress; I stand firm.
2	In God is my salvation and glory, the rock of my strength.
1,3	Trust in God at all times, O people;
4	pour out your heart before the Lord.
2	God is a refuge for us.
1	Common folk are only a breath,
2	those of rank are an illusion.
3	Placed in the scales, they rise—
4	they weigh less than a breath.
2	Put no confidence in oppression
1	nor in vain hopes or robbery.
3	Do not set your heart on riches, even when they abound.
4	Once God has spoken,
2	twice have I heard this:
1	that power belongs to God,
3	and steadfast love belongs to you, O Lord.
1	Surely you repay all according to their deeds.

4,2	Out of the depths we cry to you,
1,3	O Lord, hear our voice!
2	Listen, O Lord,
1,3,4	(Listen)
2	to the sound of our supplication!
1	If you would mark guilt, O Lord, who could stand?
3	But with you is forgiveness—we stand in awe.
4	We wait for the Lord,
1,2	our spirits wait,
4	and in God's Word we hope.
3	We wait for the Lord more than those who watch for morning
2	(more than those who watch for morning).
4	O people, hope in God!
3	For with God there is steadfast love,
2	with God is redemption aplenty.
1	It is God who will save us from all our sins.

Adapted from Psalm 62 and Psalm 130.

15. Through the Valley of the Shadow

Background

When we experience major loss and grief, faith in God sustains us as we "walk through the valley of the shadow" (Psalm 23:4). This script incorporates psalms of lament, prophetic encouragement, and apostolic exhortation to remind us of the rich resources of our faith in times of trouble.

Rehearsal Notes

This script is designed for four readers. Invite the readers to identify the different moods reflected in the various paragraphs (lament, reassurance, grief, encouragement) and to reflect that tone in their reading. The phrase "Yea, though I walk through the valley ..." is the recurring thread that ties the reading together.

Note the instructions for the "round" near the end of the reading. First, have all four readers try the line in unison in the rhythm suggested. Then rehearse it as a "round" several times, so they are comfortable with its rhythm. And don't forget the final two lines spoken by single readers.

Worship Planning

This reading can be used in a service where two or three persons are invited to reflect on their faith as a source of strength when they walked "through the valley of the shadow." In such a context, I used the following order of service:

Call to Worship (from Psalms 30 and 46)
    Leader: God is our refuge and strength, a very present help
        in time of trouble.
    People: *Therefore we will not fear, though the earth should*
        change, though the mountains shake in the heart of
        the sea. The Lord of Hosts is with us. The God of
        Jacob and Rachel is our refuge.
    Leader: Sing praises to the Lord, O you saints! Give thanks
        to God's holy name!
    People: *Lord, you have turned my mourning into dancing. You*
        have loosed my sackcloth and girded me with
        gladness. My soul will praise you and give thanks forever!

Opening Hymn   "My Life Flows On"
Readers Theater   "Through the Valley of the Shadow"
Hymn   "Shepherd Me, O God," congregation and soloist
Reflections
Prayer
Hymn   "Precious Lord, Take My Hand"
Benediction (in unison)
    May God bless you and keep you.
    May the very face of God shine on you and be gracious to you.
    May God's presence embrace you and give you peace.
Closing Song   "Benediction" (No. 16 in this book)

Through the Valley of the Shadow

1	Yea, though I walk through the valley,
2	the valley of the shadow of death,
3	O God, you are with me.
4	Your presence, my comfort and hope.

1	How long, O Lord?
2	Will you forget me forever?
1	How long will you hide your face from me?
2	How long must I bear pain in my soul, and have sorrow in my heart all the day?
1	Consider and answer me, O God.
2	Lighten my eyes lest I sleep the sleep of death.
1	I am weary with moaning; every night I flood my bed with tears;
2	my eye wastes away because of grief.
1	Yea, though I walk through the valley of the shadow of death ...

3	Fear not, I have redeemed you;
4	I have called you by name; you are mine.
3	When you pass through the waters, I will be with you;
4	through the rivers, they shall not overwhelm you.
3	When you walk through fire, you shall not be burned,
4	and the flame shall not consume you.
1	Yea, though I walk through the valley of the shadow ...
3	O God, you are with me.

2	Taking with him Peter and James and John, Jesus began to be greatly distressed and troubled.
4	"My soul is very sorrowful, even to death; remain here and watch."
2	Going a little farther, he fell on the ground and prayed that, if it were possible, the hour might pass from him. Jesus said,
4	"Abba, Father, all things are possible to you. Remove this cup from me, yet not what I will, but what you will."
1	Yea, though I walk through the valley,
4	the valley of the shadow ...

2	Fear not; I am with you.
3	Be not dismayed, for I am your God.
2	I will strengthen you, I will help you,
3	I will uphold you with my victorious right hand.
4	Your presence my comfort and hope....

1	Therefore since we are justified by faith, let us have peace with God through our Lord Jesus Christ.
2	Through him we have obtained access to the grace in which we stand.
3	And we rejoice in our hope of sharing the glory of God.
4	More than that, we rejoice in our sufferings,
1	knowing that suffering produces endurance,
2	and endurance produces character,
3	and character produces hope,
4	and hope does not disappoint us,
1	because God's love has been poured into our hearts through the Holy Spirit which has been given to us.

{The following line is chanted rhythmically as a round by four readers. Each reader reads the whole sentence, beginning when the previous reader says "walk." Each slanted line represents a beat in the rhythm. After all four readers complete the sentence, Readers 1 and 2 read the last two lines in the usual way.}

1	/ / / / / Yea, though I walk through the valley of the shadow of death,
2	/ / / / Yea, though I walk through the valley of the shadow
3,4	/ / / Yea, though I walk through the valley
1	/ / I fear no evil.
2	/ / / of death, I fear no evil.
3,4	/ / / / of the shadow of death, I fear no evil.
1	O God, you are with me;
2	your presence my comfort and hope.

Adapted from Psalms 13:1-3; 6:6-7; 23:4; Isaiah 41:10; 43:1-2; Mark 14:33-36; and Romans 5:1-5.

16. Responsive Reading on Psalm 23 and the Beatitudes

Background

There is a beautiful interplay between some of the words and themes of the Beatitudes and the twenty-third Psalm. This reading uses a different Beatitude to respond to each of the lines of Psalm 23, thus inviting reflection on the connection between the psalmist's quiet confidence in God and the blessings promised in the Sermon on the Mount.

Rehearsal Notes

While this reading is arranged as a responsive reading, it could also be formatted for two or four readers. If this is done, assign one (or two) readers to read the Beatitudes and the other(s) to read Psalm 23, so that the interplay between the two texts is preserved.

Do not rush the reading of this script. The leader (or readers) should allow a brief silence or pause after each couplet, so that the congregation can prayerfully reflect on the words and the Spirit can minister in the silence.

Worship Planning

As a response to this reading, choose a hymn that highlights either the Beatitudes or Psalm 23, such as:

> "You Are Salt for the Earth"
> "I Bind My Heart This Tide"
> "Lead Me, Lord"
> "My Shepherd Will Supply My Need"
> "Shepherd Me, O God"
> "The King of Love My Shepherd Is"

Responsive Reading on Psalm 23 and the Beatitudes

Leader: The Lord is my shepherd, I shall not want.

People: *Blessed are the poor in spirit, for theirs is the kingdom of heaven.*

Leader: The Lord makes me lie down in green pastures and leads me beside still waters.

People: *Blessed are the meek for they shall inherit the earth.*

Leader: The Lord restores my soul.

People: *Blessed are the pure in heart, for they shall see God.*

Leader: The Lord leads me in paths of righteousness for the sake of God's name.

People: *Blessed are those who hunger and thirst after righteousness, for they shall be satisfied.*

Leader: Even though I walk through the valley of the shadow of death, I fear no evil, for you are with me.

People: *Blessed are those who are persecuted for righteousness' sake, for theirs is the kingdom of God.*

Leader: Your rod and your staff—they comfort me.

People: *Blessed are those who mourn, for they shall be comforted.*

Leader: You prepare a table for me in the presence of my enemies.

People: *Blessed are the peacemakers, for they shall be called children of God.*

Leader: You anoint my head with oil; my cup overflows. Surely goodness and mercy shall follow me all the days of my life.

People: *Blessed are the merciful, for they shall obtain mercy,*

Leader: And I shall dwell in the house of the Lord forever.

People: *You are the salt of the earth. You are the light of the world.*

ALL: *Let your light so shine that all may see your good works and give glory to God.*

Old Testament Readings

17. What Do These Stones Mean?

18. Micah 6: A Dramatic Paraphrase

19. Seek the Lord: Micah and the Prophets

20. Behold! I Make All Things New!

21. A Heart of Wisdom

17. What Do These Stones Mean?

Background

This script uses the story of Joshua 4:1-7 as the narrative context to explore faith as an edifice of "living stones." Joshua invites the tribes to gather literal stones as a symbol of their faith journey, so that the next generation will see the stones and hear the story of God's redemptive work. The New Testament texts (1 Corinthians 3:10-11 and 1 Peter 2:4-10) extend this symbolism to Christ and the church: believers are "living stones" built on the foundation of Christ. Introducing and closing this reflection is a prayer of praise (based on Psalm 90:1, 17) which acknowledges God's faithfulness from generation to generation.

Rehearsal Notes

The script is for four readers. The opening and closing exhortation are the "envelope" into which the other texts fit. Invite the readers to speak with enthusiasm, as if the congregation will be hearing these words for the first time.

At those points where several readers read together, they may be tempted to speak more softly, but the point of multiple voices is to increase the volume and emphasis. Rehearse these sections until readers feel comfortable with a common rhythm.

Worship Planning

This reading could be used in a service where three or four people are each invited to speak for three to four minutes on a person who has been a "living stone" for him or her. Invite each speaker to describe the person, or relate an experience that shows how that person was a testimony of faith. Then use the following sequence to introduce this part of the service:

Readers Theater	"What Do These Stones Mean?"
Hymn	"Living Stones" (*Sing and Rejoice!* No. 60)
	or "Christ Is Our Cornerstone"

Reflections on "Living Heritage... Living Stones... We Remember,"
        by three or four persons

Congregational Response
    Leader: What do these stones mean?
                What do these living stones mean?
    People: *The Lord has been our dwelling place in all generations.*
                We rejoice in the living heritage that is ours!
    Leader: The foundation is already laid ... Jesus Christ our Lord.
    People: *Living heritage! Living stones! Let us all take care*
                how we build!

Prayer or Closing Hymn   "The Church's One Foundation"

The congregational response is used after each of the three or four reflections. This becomes a way for the congregation to exhort each other as well as respond to what they have just heard. Before the reflections, a leader should introduce the topic briefly and explain the congregational response.

What Do These Stones Mean?

1	Lord, you have been our dwelling place in all generations!
2	And the favor of the Lord has rested upon us!
3	God has established the work of our hands.
4	One generation playing its part and passing on;
2	Another generation playing its part and passing on.
1,3	Lord, you have been our dwelling place in all generations!
4	And when the people had crossed the Jordan, the Lord said to Joshua,
1	"Take twelve people, and take twelve stones from the midst of the Jordan. Carry these stones with you to the place where you will stay."
4	And Joshua called the twelve people,
2	"Each of you take a stone and carry it with you. We will set them up in the place where we stay. And this shall be a sign among you: In days to come, your children will come to you, and when they shall ask, 'What do these stones mean?'
1	(What do these stones mean?)
3	(What do these living stones mean?)
2	Then you shall tell them how the Lord has been our dwelling place in this generation.
1	So these stones will be a memorial forever—
3	a living heritage to all generations."
4	One generation playing its part and passing on.
2	Another generation playing its part and passing on.
3	What do these stones mean?
1	What do these living stones mean?
3	Others, by the grace of God, have laid the foundation, and now we build upon it.
2	For no other foundation can anyone lay, than that which is laid—namely, Jesus Christ.
4	Others, by the grace of God, have laid the foundation, and now we build upon it.
1	But let each one take care how she builds!
3	Let each one take care how he builds!

4	One generation playing its part and passing on.
2	Another generation playing its part and passing on.
1	What do these stones mean?
2	What do these living stones mean?
3	Come to the Lord, to that Living Stone!
2	Rejected by the world, but chosen by God.
1	Come to that Living Stone!
4	And be yourselves like living stones,
1	built into a house to the glory of God!
2	A chosen race, a royal priesthood, a holy nation, God's own people!
1,3	You are living stones!
1	Built into a living heritage to the glory of God!
4	To declare the wonderful deeds of God who has called you out of darkness into marvelous light!
1,2,3,4	You are living stones!
3	Once you were no people; now you are God's people!
2	Once "you had no experience of mercy, now it is intimately yours!"[6]
1	Come to that Living Stone!
2	Come to that Cornerstone!
3	And be yourselves like living stones—
1,4	Take care how you build!
1	Lord, you have been our dwelling place in all generations!
2	And the favor of the Lord has rested upon us!
3	God has established the work of our hands.
4	One generation playing its part and passing on;
2	Another generation playing its part and passing on.
1	Living heritage—
2	living stones!
3	What do these stones mean?
4	What do these living stones mean?

[6]The New Testament in Modern English, translated by J. B. Phillips. New York: Macmillan, 1958.

Adapted from Joshua 4:1-7; Psalm 90:1, 17; 1 Corinthians 3:10-11; 1 Peter 2:4-10; and two lines from a poem by Walt Whitman.

18. Micah 6: A Dramatic Paraphrase

Background

Micah 6:1-8 announces a "lawsuit" by God against the people of Israel. This script adopts a court-room setting to present and update this text, dramatizing the underlying humor and drama of the prophet's word. The modern audience is drawn into the interrogation of God's people: What does the Lord require of us? Many interpreters have found Micah's answer to be a succinct summary of biblical faith: do justly, love mercy, walk humbly with your God.

Rehearsal Notes

This script is for four readers. Note the introductory instructions. The opening "pivot" should be rehearsed until it happens smoothly. Establish an upbeat tempo immediately: the first eight speeches should occur quickly. Encourage the readers to exaggerate slightly the drama (and humor) of the lines. When "God" begins to "testify," the intensity levels off only to build again, during the "people's" long speech. This speech should begin pensively and build excitement until the "prophet" interrupts.

If your circumstances permit, try this staging with the repeating lines at the end ("do what is just, show constant love, walk humbly with your God"): as the "prophet," "mountains," and "God" each say their lines for the *second* time, they walk to a seat in the audience. Each delivers their lines for the third time while standing at their seat. Thus, the "People" are left in front alone at the end. Again, rehearse until it occurs smoothly.

You will need to adapt the script for your circumstance in two places. First, an early speech mentions "the flint hills," a feature of Kansas geography. Substitute an appropriate term for your locale: foothills, Black Hills, Appalachian hills, etc. The second place occurs during the listing of the leaders (Moses, Miriam, etc.). I added humor to this "God" speech by including other "M" names—Mary, Martha, Menno (Simons), Martin (Luther)—and then ending with the name of a prominent local leader the audience would know. Again, adapt for your setting.

Worship Planning

This script can be used in a service where Micah 6:1-8 is the theme. In such a service, I used the following sequence to present the Old Testament and New Testament readings:

Old Testament Lesson
Scripture Reading	Micah 6:1-8
Dramatic Paraphrase	"Micah 6:1-8: A Dramatic Paraphrase"
Hymn	"Micah" (No. 7 in this book)

New Testament Lesson
Scripture Reading	Matthew 5:1-16
Song	"Lead Me, Lord" (first time—soloist; second time—congregation)

The song "Micah" has the flavor of a folk song. If you want a hymn, you might consider "What Does the Lord Require?" which has a decidedly different tone. I chose the Beatitudes from Matthew as Jesus' statement of what God "requires" or blesses; you can either have someone read the Scripture or read it responsively. "Lead Me, Lord" is a lovely refrain that deserves to be sung twice; you might have a soloist sing it first and the congregation repeat it.

Micah 6: A Dramatic Paraphrase

{Four readers line up on stage, backs to the audience, in this order: God, Mountains, Prophet, People. A fifth person reads Micah 6:1-8 from the Bible. As soon as the last verse is read, the four readers turn to face the audience and the prophet begins speaking.}

Prophet:	Hear ye, hear ye! Court is now in session!
God:	The Lord God is bringing a lawsuit against God's people!
People:	What kind of court? Who are the witnesses?
Prophet:	The universe is the courtroom, the whole earth is judge and jury! Arise! Plead your case before the mountains!
Mountains:	Wait a minute! As mountains, we are busy with wildlife and forest right now. I'm not sure we have time for this!
Prophet:	Let the hills hear your voice!
Mountains:	Well, if the flint hills can listen, so can we!
Prophet:	Hear, mountains! Listen, earth—all the way to China! The Lord has a complaint against this people. The Lord is suing this people! Court is now in session! God versus the people. State your case!
God:	Oh, my people, my people—what have I done to you? How have I burdened you? Answer me!
People:	Is that God speaking? Who ever heard of God suing anyone?
God:	I brought you out of slavery, out of Egypt —and Ohio, Pennsylvania, and Kansas.
Mountains:	God has a point there.
God:	I sent you leaders: Moses, Miriam, Mary, Martha, Menno, Martin—Harold—and many more!
People:	What can we say? How can we answer these charges?
God:	Remember how you were afraid you would be cursed with failure, but instead I blessed you with many good things?
People:	So what do you want from us now?
God:	Haven't I gone with you on this journey all the way? How have I burdened you? Answer me?
People:	How shall we come to the Lord? What can we do? Shall we sacrifice goats and rams? Will the Lord be pleased with 10,000 barrels of oil? *{a dawning idea}* We'll take up a big offering! Let's get the choir to sing! We'll make everyone come to church! We'll preach and we'll pray and we'll sing—! *{interrupting}*
Prophet:	STOP!
God:	God has shown you, O people, what is good ...

People:	What is this? The verdict or the sentence?
Prophet:	You know what the Lord requires of you!
People:	Is that a threat?
Prophet:	Do what is just.
Mountains:	Show constant love.
God:	Walk humbly with your God.
People:	Is that a requirement?
Prophet:	Do what is just.
Mountains:	Show constant love.
God:	Walk humbly with your God.
People:	Or a blessing?
Prophet:	Do what is just.
Mountains:	Show constant love.
God:	Walk humbly with your God.
People:	Court adjourned.

19. Seek the Lord: Micah and the Prophets

Background

Micah 6:8 is the organizing theme for presenting the message of the eighth-century prophets—Amos, Hosea, Isaiah, and Micah. Amos preaches to "do justly," while "love mercy" is at the heart of Hosea's preaching. Isaiah counsels, "Walk humbly with your God."

Undergirding the reading are the questions: What does it mean to seek the Lord? What does the Lord require of us? The Hebrew word for seek and the Hebrew word for require are the same word. The script also draws on Jesus' prophetic words and portions of the Psalms.

Rehearsal Notes

This script is for four readers. Each reader speaks for one of the prophetic figures: Amos, Hosea, Isaiah, or Jesus. Invite the readers to speak with fervor—to "become" the prophets. Ask them to imagine that the congregation is hearing these words for the first time.

Note the suggestions in the script for staging the ending. Feel free to adapt to your setting.

Worship Planning

Psalm 146 makes a wonderful call to worship for a service focusing on prophetic themes; "Sing Praise to God Who Reigns" complements the psalm as an opening hymn of praise.

The "Micah" song (No. 7 in this book) works well as a response to the readers theater. Consider the following as a benediction and conclude with "Benediction" (No. 16 in this book):

> Benediction
>
> Leader: Seek the Lord and live!
>
> *People: We seek God's presence in our lives and in our world.*
>
> Leader: Hold fast to love and justice; wait continually for your God.
>
> *People: We seek to be channels of peace and rivers flowing with God's truth and righteousness.*
>
> Leader: Go forth and live as God's goodness requires: do justly, love mercy, walk humbly with God.

Seek the Lord: Micah and the Prophets

1   Make a joyful noise to the Lord!

2   Serve the Lord with gladness!

3   God is our refuge and strength!

4   Know that the Lord is God!

1   The Psalmist says, "Seek the Lord and the Lord's strength.
Seek God's presence continually."

2   The prophet Isaiah says, "Seek the Lord while the Lord may be
found. Call upon God while God is near."

3   The prophet Amos says, "Seek the Lord and live. Love the good.
Establish justice in the gate. Seek the Lord and live."

4   And Jesus says, "Seek first the Kingdom of God,
God's justice and righteousness. You will have all you need."

1   Seek the Lord!

2   Seek the Lord!

3   But what does the Lord require of us?

4   What does the Lord seek from us?

3   The prophet Micah says, "God has shown you, O people, what is good."
And this is what the Lord seeks from you:
Do justly, love mercy, walk humbly with your God.

1   Do justly,

2   love mercy,

4   walk humbly with your God.

1   Thus says the Lord through the prophet Amos:
Do justly! Do justly!
You who sell the righteous for silver, the needy for shoes!
You who trample the poor in the dust and turn away the afflicted.
Do justly! Let justice roll down like waters
and righteousness like an everflowing stream!

3   Do justly,

2   love mercy,

4   walk humbly with your God.

2   Thus says the Lord through the prophet Hosea:
Love mercy! Love mercy!
When Israel was a child, I loved him!
Out of Egypt I called my son!
And the more I called them, the more they worshiped other gods!
Yet it was I—I who taught Ephraim to walk!
I took him in my arms!
I led them with cords of compassion and with bands of love.

{in anger}
But my people are bent on turning away from me!
The swords shall rage against their cities!
{now compassionately}
How can I give you up, O Ephraim?
How can I hand you over? My heart moves within me!
My compassion grows warm and tender!
I will not carry out my fierce anger. I will not destroy
Ephraim!
For I am God—not a human being!
I am the Holy One in your midst—I will not come to destroy!

1	Do justly,
2	love mercy,
3	walk humbly with your God.

4   Thus says the Lord through the prophet Isaiah:
Walk humbly. Walk humbly with your God.
In returning and rest, you shall be saved.
In quietness and trust shall be your strength.
But you would not! You said, "No! We will speed away on horses!"
Therefore, you will speed away—as you run away!
You said, "We ride on swift horses!"
Therefore, your pursuers will ride swift horses!
Yet the Lord waits to be gracious to you!
The Lord waits to be gracious to you!
God rises up to show you compassion.
For the Lord is a God of justice!
Blessed are all those who wait upon the Lord!
Walk humbly, walk humbly with your God.

1	Do justly,
2	love mercy,
4	walk humbly with your God.

3   Jesus says, "The Spirit of the Lord is upon me.
Because God has anointed me to preach good news to the poor.
God has sent me to proclaim release to the captives,
recovery of sight to the blind.
To set free those who are oppressed."
This is the kingdom of God!
And this is what the Lord seeks from you:
Seek first God's kingdom, God's justice and righteousness,
and you will have all you need!

3   Seek first God's kingdom:

1   do justly,

2   love mercy,

4   walk humbly with your God!

{As these last lines are repeated for a second and third time, the readers walk to four seats scattered throughout the congregation, or to points surrounding the congregation. They reach these spots just before they read their lines for the final time.}

3   Seek first God's kingdom:

1   do justly,

2   love mercy,

4   walk humbly with your God!

3   Seek first God's kingdom:

1   do justly,

2   love mercy,

4   walk humbly with your God!

Adapted from Psalms 100:1-2; 46:1; 105:4; Micah 6:8; Isaiah 55:6-7; 30:15-18; Amos 5:4, 14-15, 24; 2:6-7; Hosea 11:1-4, 7, 8-9; Luke 4:18-21; and Matthew 6:33.

20. Behold! I Make All Things New!

Background

The biblical God is a God of new beginnings. The God of the exodus does a "new thing" in bringing the people out of exile (Isaiah 43:15-21). The One who sits on the throne at the end of history declares, "Behold, I make all things new!" (Revelation 21:5). Paul declares that those who are in Christ have become new creatures (2 Corinthians 5:17-20). This script draws all these texts into an urgent and energetic call from the God who would renew humanity and the world.

Rehearsal Notes

This script is structured for two readers. The opening paragraph occurs four times throughout the reading; each time it should be read with energy and clarity. Rehearse the sections where the two readers speak together; the intent is to increase volume and intensity in those places. The readers can evoke this sense of the "new thing" God is doing by the way in which they read. Encourage each other to speak with enthusiasm and anticipation—as if hearing and speaking these words for the first time!

Worship Planning

As a call to worship, use some of the Psalms that speak of singing a "new song," such as Psalms 96 and 98. The song "New Earth, Heavens New" is a fitting response to the readers theater script. The vision in Revelation 21:1-5 would make a fitting benediction.

Behold! I Make All Things New!

1	Behold!
2	Behold!
1	I am doing a new thing!
2	Now it springs forth! Don't you see it?
1	Behold!
2	Behold!
1,2	I make all things new!

1	I am the Lord God, your Holy One,
2	the Creator of the world, and Redeemer of my people.
1	I made a way in the sea, a path in the mighty waters.
2	The horse and chariot were extinguished, the army and warrior quenched like a wick!
1	Remember not the former things,
2	nor consider the things of old—

1	Behold!
2	Behold!
1	I am doing a new thing!
2	Now it springs forth! Don't you see it?
1	Behold!
2	Behold!
1,2	I make all things new!

2	The former things have come to pass!
1	And new things I now declare:
2	not a way in the sea—
1	(exodus out of Egypt)
2	but a way in the wilderness
1	(escape from exile!)
2	From Babylon to Zion, I will bring back my people
1	that they might declare my praise!
2	A voice cries:
1	In the wilderness, prepare the way of the Lord!
2	Lift up every valley!
1	Level the mountains!
2	Smooth the rough places!
1,2	For all flesh shall see the glory of God!

1	Behold!
2	Behold!
1	I am doing a new thing!
2	Now it springs forth! Don't you see it?
1	Behold!
2	Behold!
1,2	I make all things new!

2	If anyone is in Christ, there is a new creation.
1	The old has passed away. Behold the new has come.
2	All this is from God, who through Christ, reconciled us to God's self,
1	and gave to us the ministry of reconciliation.
2	So we are ambassadors for Christ, God making appeal through us.
1	Ambassadors for Christ, God making appeal through us.
2	A people created to declare God's praise.
1	The former things have come to pass!
2	And new things God now declares:

1	Behold!
2	Behold!
1	I am doing a new thing!
2	Now it springs forth! Don't you see it?
1	Behold!
2	Behold!
1,2	I make all things new!

Adapted from Isaiah 43:15-21; 40:3-5; Revelation 21:5; and 2 Corinthians 5:17-20.

21. A Heart of Wisdom

Background

The theme of this reading on wisdom is the prayer in Psalm 90:12: "So teach us to number our days that we may get a heart of wisdom." The script begins with excerpts from Psalm 145 and Proverbs 3 that extol the wisdom of God in creating and redeeming the world. Portions of the Wisdom of Solomon, an apocryphal book, describe the nature of wisdom and echo her desirability as an object of human pursuit. Finally, the reflection concludes with an adaptation of Paul's words in Philippians 4:8-9.

Rehearsal Notes

This script is for four readers. Carefully rehearse the places where several readers speak together to increase volume and intensity. Practice these sections until readers sense a common cadence and can read together easily.

Worship Planning

This reading would fit into a service whose theme is the pursuit of wisdom. It could also be used to highlight Christian education in the church or to celebrate graduation or opening-of-school events. The hymn "Be Thou My Vision" is an appropriate congregational response to this readers theater piece; it continues the prayerful tone of Psalm 90:12.

A Heart of Wisdom

1	Great is the Lord and greatly to be praised!
2	God's greatness is unsearchable!
3	One generation shall laud God's works to another
4	and declare God's mighty acts.
1,2,3,4	Great is the Lord and greatly to be praised!

1	God founded the earth by wisdom;
2	established the heavens by understanding.
3	The Lord bestows wisdom and teaches knowledge and understanding.
4	Great is the Lord and greatly to be praised!
2	Happy are those who find wisdom and those who get understanding,
3	for her income is better than silver,
4	and her revenue better than gold.
1	Teach us, O God, to number our days that we may get a heart of wisdom.

3	The beginning of wisdom is the most sincere desire for instruction,
4	and concern for instruction is love of her,
2	and love of her is the keeping of the laws,
1	and giving heed to her laws is assurance of immortality,
2	and immortality brings one near to God;
3	so the desire of wisdom leads to a kingdom.
1,4	Teach us, O God, to number our days that we may get a heart of wisdom.

2	There is in wisdom a spirit that is intelligent, holy,
3	unique, manifold, subtle,
4	mobile, clear, unpolluted,
1	distinct, invulnerable, loving the good,
3	keen, irresistible, beneficent,
4	humane, steadfast, sure,
2	free from anxiety, all-powerful, overseeing all.
1	For wisdom is more mobile than any motion;
2	because of her pureness she pervades and penetrates all things.
3	She is a breath of the power of God,
4	and a pure emanation of the glory of the Almighty.

2	She is a reflection of eternal light,
3	a spotless mirror of the working of God,
1	an image of God's goodness.

4	Though she is but one, she can do all things,
1	and while remaining in herself, she renews all things.
2,3	In every generation
3	she passes into holy souls and makes them friends of God and prophets;
2	for God loves nothing so much as the person who lives with wisdom.
1,3,4	Teach us, O God, to number our days that we may get a heart of wisdom.

2	So, brothers and sisters,
1	whatever is true,
3	whatever is honorable,
4	whatever is just,
1	whatever is pure,
2	whatever is gracious,
3	if there is any excellence,
4	if there is anything worthy of praise,
1,2,3,4	think about these things.
2	What you have learned and received and heard and seen—do;
1	and the God of all peace and wisdom will be with you.

1,2,3,4	Teach us, O God, to number our days, that we may get a heart of wisdom.

Adapted from Psalms 145:3; 90:12; Proverbs 3:13-14, 19-20; Wisdom of Solomon 6:17-20; 7:22-28; and Philippians 4:8-9.

The Parables of Matthew 13

22. What Is New, What Is Old
23. Parable of the Sower
24. Mystery and Growth
25. Weeds and Harvest

22. What Is New, What Is Old

Background

The presentation of seven parables in Matthew 13 ends with Jesus saying, "Every scribe who has been trained for the kingdom of heaven is like a householder who brings out of his treasure what is new and what is old." Incorporating texts from Isaiah, Psalms, and Philippians, this reading explores the value of the new and the old in the dynamic of faith. We seek to respect the tradition and the new creation unfolding—and to discern in both God's truth.

This script could be combined with a reading of the parables of the treasure and the pearl (Matthew 13:44-46) which involve people trading all they have ("the old") for something "new" which is more valuable.

Rehearsal Notes

This script is for four readers. Notice that Matthew 13:52 is repeated four times; each time it should be spoken with deliberateness and emphasis. The other scriptural references and the simple poetry are intended to interpret the Matthew verse. Each Scripture passage values either the "new" or the "old," thus presenting a contrast with what precedes or follows it. Readers should try to show this variation by their tone of voice.

Worship Planning

This reading could be used in a single service with the theme "Treasuring What is New and What is Old." It could also be used as the first service in a four-part series on the parables in Matthew 13: (1) What Is New, What Is Old; (2) Parable of the Sower; (3) Mystery and Growth; (4) Weeds and Harvest. Given the agricultural images, such a series might work best during the summer or early fall.

In the worship service, follow this reading by singing two hymns: the first, a hymn new to your congregation and the second, an old hymn representing the familiar, the traditional. Call the first hymn "A Hymn for New Beginnings" and the second "A Hymn for Valuing Our Heritage."

> Possibilities for "new" hymns:
> "New Earth, Heavens New"
> "Earth and All Stars"
> "This Is a Day of New Beginnings"
> "Mothering God, You Gave Me Birth"
> Possibilities for "old" hymns:
> "O God, Our Help in Ages Past"
> "I Love to Tell the Story"
> "Great Is Thy Faithfulness"

The purpose of these two hymns is to present a vivid contrast between "what is new, what is old," so choose the hymns carefully to accentuate the range. If the suggested "new songs" are already familiar to your congregation, choose a third that represents a challenge! The "traditional" hymn should evoke memories of an earlier generation and might be considered "old-fashioned" by some. A sermon or reflections could pursue how the "treasure" of our faith involves incorporating both the old and the new.

What Is New, What Is Old

1   Every scribe who has become a learner in the kingdom of God
      is like a householder who brings out of his treasure
      what is new and what is old.

1   What is new ... what is old ...

2   Sing a new song! Tell the old, old story!

3   discovering the new, preserving the old,

4   finding in both what is dross, what is gold.

2   Remember not the former things, nor consider the things of old!
      Behold I am doing a new thing!
      Now it springs forth—don't you see it?

3   Remember the former things! Consider the things of old!
      for I am God and there is no other,
      declaring the end from the beginning
      and from ancient times, things not yet done.

4   Every scribe who has become a learner in the kingdom of God
      is like a householder who brings out of her treasure
      what is old and what is new.

1   What is old! What is new!

2   To be faithful ... to be open ...

3   interpreting the old, discerning the new,

4   choosing in both what is good and true.

1   I remember the days of old. I meditate on all God has done.
      I muse on what God's hand has wrought.
      Teach me, O God, the way I should go, for to you I lift up my soul.

4   Behold, I create new heavens and a new earth!
      The former things shall not be remembered or come into mind!
      Be glad! Rejoice forever in what I create!

2   Every scribe who has become a learner in the kingdom of God
      is like a householder who brings out of his treasure
      what is new and what is old.

1   What is new! What is old!

2   Ongoing study, ongoing search,

3   applying the old in a new situation.

4   Respect for tradition and new creation.

4   Not that I am already perfect, but one thing I do:
forgetting what lies behind and straining forward to what lies
ahead, I press on toward the goal for the prize
of the upward call of God in Christ Jesus.

3   Every scribe who is a learner in the kingdom
is like a householder who takes out of her treasure
what is new and what is old.

Adapted from Matthew 13:52; Isaiah 43:18; 46:8-10; 65:17-18; Psalm 143:5, 8; and Philippians 3:12-14.

23. Parable of the Sower

Background

This reading presents the parable of the sower incorporating teachings from Jeremiah and James that use the same planting metaphor. The repetition of "the sower went out to sow ..." in the script emphasizes that the act of responding fruitfully to God's Word does not occur only once, but over and over again in our daily living. The Spirit continues to sow the seeds of God's truth, and we are challenged to cultivate the soil of our lives in ways that produce a harvest of righteousness.

Rehearsal Notes

The script is designed for four readers. The opening paragraph ("A sower went out to sow ...") is repeated in several forms in the reading.

These lines should be read in a rhythmic style following the beat given below:

```
    /               /               /
A sower went out to sow his seed, and as he sowed,
    /
and as he sowed,
    /                    /
What are the ears with which you hear?
    /                /
What do you hear? What do you hear?
    /                /
Listen.          Listen.
```

Rehearse this until readers develop a clear rhythm of reading. The other parts of the script can be read in more normal voice, thus creating a pattern of alternating rhythmic and free-style reading.

Worship Planning

This reading could be used in a single service on the Parable of the Sower or as part of a series on the parables of Matthew 13. (See worship notes for Reading 22, "What Is New, What Is Old.") Incorporate other New Testament texts mentioning spiritual fruitfulness and seed-related metaphors such as John 15; John 12:24-26; or 1 Peter 1:22-25. Hymn possibilities include:

"We Plow the Fields and Scatter"
"Thou True Vine, That Heals"
"You Are Salt for the Earth"
"Seed, Scattered and Sown"

Consider the following benediction and closing hymn. The adage "Mighty things from small beginnings grow" is a quotation attributed to J. Dryden in a long-forgotten quotations collection.

Benediction
Leader: What kind of seeds? What kind of soil?
People: *We go forth, rooted and grounded in love, ready to sow*
             seeds that will bear fruit in holiness.
Leader: Go forth, believing that God can make mighty things from
             small beginnings grow.
People: *We go, trusting in God to give life to the seed.*
Closing Hymn   "God Is Working His Purpose Out"

Parable of the Sower

1	A sower went out to sow his seed, and as he sowed
2	and as he sowed ...
3	What are the ears with which you hear?
4	What do you hear?
2	What do you hear?
1	Listen.
	{pause}
2	Listen.
1	A sower went out to sow his seed, and as he sowed
2	and as he sowed ...
3	Some seed fell along the path and birds came and devoured it.
2	Other seed fell on rocky ground where it had not much soil. Immediately it sprang up. But the sun rose and scorched it. It withered away.
1	A sower went out to sow his seed, and as he sowed
2	and as he sowed ...
4	other seed fell among the thorns, and the thorns grew up and choked it. It yielded no grain.
2	Is this the world?
1	Soil and seeds!
3	Birds devouring,
2	sun scorching,
4	thorns choking.
2	Is this the world?
3	What kind of soil?
4	What kind of seeds?
1	Listen!
	{pause}
2	Listen!
1	A sower went out to sow his seed, and as he sowed,
2	and as he sowed ...
1	Other seeds fell into good soil and brought forth grain growing up, increasing and yielding thirtyfold,
1,2	sixtyfold,
1,2,3,4	a hundredfold.

2   Is this the world?

4   Soil and seeds ...

1   growing up, increasing and yielding ...

2   Is this the world?

4   All kinds of soil! All kinds of seeds!

3   Along the path,

2   on rocky ground,

4   among the thorns,

1   into good soil.

3   What are the ears with which you hear?

4   What do you hear?

2   What do you hear?

1   Listen.

     {pause}

2   Listen.

1   Everyone who hears God's Word and does it,
     I will tell you what he is like:

2   He is like a tree planted by water,
     that sends out its roots by the stream,

3   that does not fear when scorching heat comes,
     for its leaves remain green;

4   and it is not anxious in the year of drought,
     for it does not cease to bear fruit.

3   What are the ears with which you hear?

4   What do you hear?

2   What do you hear?

1   Listen.

     {pause}

2   Listen.

3   Is there any among you who is wise? By her good life,
     let her show her works in the meekness of wisdom.

2   But if you have seeds of bitter jealousy and selfish ambition in
     your hearts, this is not the wisdom that comes down from above.

4   It will yield what is earthbound, unspiritual, demonic.

1	But the harvest of righteousness is sown in peace by those who make peace.
2	And the wisdom from above is first pure,
3	then peaceable, gentle, open to reason and truth,
4	full of mercy and good fruits.
1	Cultivate these things and you sow seeds that will bear fruit in holiness.
2	Cultivate these things and you sow seeds that will bear fruit in holiness.
1	A sower went out to sow his seed, and as he sowed
2	and as he sowed ...
3	What are the ears with which you hear?
4	What do you hear?
2	What do you hear?
1	Listen.
	{pause}
2	Listen.

Adapted from Matthew 13:3-9; Jeremiah 17:7-8; and James 3:13-18.

24. Mystery and Growth

Background

This reading focuses on the parables in Matthew 13 which highlight the mystery and hidden-ness of the kingdom (the mustard seed and the leaven), and it incorporates a parable from Mark 4 about the seed growing secretly. These parables remind us that the ways of the kingdom often involve imperceptible growth and are still largely a mystery to the human mind.

Rehearsal Notes

This script is for four readers. The reading presents three parables with a recurring refrain ("Mystery, wonder, hiddenness, growth"), an expanding commentary, and a developing prayer: "O God, grant that we may understand the mystery of the kingdom."

Encourage readers to use a dramatic, storytelling tone as they read the parables and a more reflective tone as they repeat the refrain.

Worship Planning

This reading may be used in a single service whose theme is "The Mystery and Growth of the Kingdom of God," or as part of a series on the parables in Matthew 13. (See the worship notes for Reading 22, "What Is New, What Is Old.") Consider the following sequence for the opening of a worship service:

Call to Worship (from Psalm 36:5-9 and Romans 11:33)
> Leader: O God, in mystery and silence you are present in our lives: sustaining the world, creating new life, nurturing growth.
> *People: Your constant love extends to the heavens, your faithfulness to the clouds. Your justice is like the lofty mountains, your judgments like the great deep.*
> Leader: All living things are dependent on your care.
> *People: The people of earth take refuge in the shadow of your wings. For with you is the fountain of life and in your light we see light.*
> Leader: O the depth of the riches and wisdom and knowledge of God! How unsearchable God's judgments! How untraceable God's ways!
> *People: Source, Guide, and Goal of all that is—to God be glory forever!*

Hymn	"Immortal, Invisible, God Only Wise"
Readers Theater	"Mystery and Growth"
Hymn	"The Kingdom of God"

Mystery and Growth

1   Mystery ...

2   wonder ...

3   hiddenness ...

4   growth ...

3   To you it has been given to know the secrets of the kingdom!

1   Mystery ...

2   wonder ...

3   hiddenness ...

4   growth ...

1   And Jesus told this parable:

2   The reign of God is like a grain of mustard seed:
which a man took and sowed in his field.
It is the smallest of seeds, but when it has grown,
it is the greatest of shrubs, and becomes a tree.
The birds of the air come and make nests in its branches.

3   (The smallest of seeds, but the greatest of trees).

1   Mystery ...

2   wonder ...

3   hiddenness ...

4   growth ...

2   To you it has been given to know the secrets of the kingdom!

1   Mystery ...

2   wonder ...

3   hiddenness ...

4   growth ...

1   And Jesus told this parable:

3   The kingdom of God is like a lump of leaven,
which a woman took and hid in her flour.
And the yeast is hidden, but the whole loaf is leavened.
And the bread feeds the hungry.

1   Mystery ...

2   wonder ...

3   hiddenness ...

4   growth.

3   The smallest seed!

1   The hidden yeast!

4   O God, grant that we may know the secrets of the kingdom!

1	And Jesus told this parable:
4	The reign of God is as if a person scatters seed upon the ground,
	and sleeps and rises, night and day.
	And the seed sprouts and grows, he knows not how!
1	(And the seed sprouts and grows, she knows not how!)
4	The earth makes the plants grow and bear fruit:
	first the blade, and then the head,
	and then the head full of grain!
	But when the grain is ripe,
	we pick up the sickle for the harvest has come!
1	Mystery ...
2	wonder ...
3	hiddenness ...
4	growth!
3	The smallest seed!
4	The hidden yeast!
4	We know it grows, we know not how!
1	Mystery ...
2	wonder ...
3	hiddenness ...
4	growth!
2	O God, grant that we may understand the mystery of the kingdom.

Adapted from Matthew 13:31-33 and Mark 4:26-29.

25. Weeds and Harvest

Background

This final reading based on Matthew 13 picks up two different impulses in Scripture related to the "harvest": the first is the urgency to begin the ingathering (Mark 4:26-29); the second is the injunction to let both wheat and weeds grow together and to wait for the Lord of the harvest (Matthew 13:24-30 and James 5:7-9).

Rehearsal Notes

This script is for four readers. It presents three scriptural texts dealing with the harvest. Brief commands sprinkled throughout the reading highlight two possible choices: either to "pick up the sickle" or to patiently wait for God's harvesttime. Readers should try to make this contrast clear by the way they read.

Worship Planning

This reading can be used in a single service focused on "Weeds and Harvest" or as part of a series based on the parables of Matthew 13. (See worship notes for Reading 22, "What Is New, What Is Old.")

Consider the following opening order of service. Singing hymns of "judgment and mercy" back-to-back heightens the dialogue between the two points of view presented in the Scripture.

Call to Worship (from Psalms 67 and 126)

Leader:	O God, be gracious unto us and bless us and cause your face to shine upon us; that your way may be known upon the earth.
People:	*Let the people praise you, God!* *Let all the people praise you!*
Leader:	Let those who sow in tears reap with shouts of joy! Let those who go forth carrying the seed for sowing come back singing for joy as they bring in the harvest.
People:	*Let the people praise you, God! Let all the people praise you!*
Leader:	The earth shall yield its increase, and God will bless us.
People:	*Let all the ends of the earth sing to the Lord of the Harvest.*

Hymn	"Sing to the Lord of Harvest"
Readers Theater	"Weeds and Harvest"
Hymns of Judgment and Mercy	
	"Come Ye Thankful People"
	"There's a Wideness in God's Mercy"

Weeds and Harvest

1   The reign of God is as if a person scatters seed upon the
     ground,
     and sleeps and rises, night and day.

2   And the seed sprouts and grows, she knows not how;

3   The earth makes the plants grow and bear fruit:

4   first the blade, and then the head, and then the head full of grain!

1   But when the grain is ripe, she picks up the sickle
     for the harvest has come!

2   Let us pick up the sickle, for the harvest is come!

3   Let both grow together!

4   Wait for the Lord of the harvest!

3   The reign of God is like a sower who sowed good seed in his field,

4   but while everyone was sleeping, an enemy came
     and sowed weeds among the wheat and went away.

3   When the plants grew and the heads of grain began to form,
     the weeds appeared also.

2   The sower's servants said, "It was good seed you sowed in your field!
     Where did the weeds come from?"

1   "Do you want us to go and pull up the weeds?"

2   "Let us pick up the sickle, for the harvest has come!"

3   But the sower said, "No! Because as you gather the weeds,
     you might pull up some of the wheat along with them.
     Let both grow together, until the harvest.

4   Wait for the harvest.

3   And at harvesttime, I will tell the reapers, 'gather the weeds first;
     tie them in bundles to be burned, but gather the wheat into my barn.'"

2   Let us pick up the sickle, for the harvest is come!

3   Let both grow together!

4   Wait for the Lord of the harvest!

1   Be patient, therefore, brothers and sisters,
     until the coming of the Lord.
     Behold, the farmer waits for the precious fruit of the earth,
     being patient until it receives the early and the late rain.

4   Wait patiently and let your hearts stand firm.

2   Do not judge one another, that you may not be judged.
     Behold, the judge is standing at the doors!

3   For as you judge others, so you yourselves will be judged!

2   And whatever measure you deal out to others will be dealt back
     to you!

1	Be patient, brothers and sisters,
4	Seek first God's kingdom and God's righteousness,
2	cultivate the wisdom from above, which is pure, peaceable, and gentle,
3	open to reason and truth, full of mercy and good fruits.
1	Cultivate these things and you sow seeds that will bear fruit in holiness.
2	Let us pick up the sickle, for the harvest is come!
3	Let both grow together!
4	Wait for the Lord of the harvest!

Adapted from Matthew 13:24-30; 6:33; 7:1-2; Mark 4:26-29; and James 3:17-18; 5:7-9.

Gospel Readings

26. The People Who Walk in Darkness
27. Ancient Advent Songs
28. A Perceptive Story
29. Ask, Seek, Knock
30. A Thanksgiving Reading
31. "Who Am I?" The Suffering One, The Transfigured One
32. Christ as King and Christ as Servant
33. The Spirit of God (Reading 1)
34. The Spirit of God (Reading 2)
35. With Thanksgiving

26. The People Who Walk in Darkness

Background

The prophetic hope of Advent is that the people who wait in darkness will see God's light (Isaiah 9:2). So we wait for God "more than those who watch for morning" (Psalm 130). In this spirit, we hear Jesus' words to "take heed and watch" (Mark 13:33), for we don't know the precise time of his coming. This reading gathers up these three texts to express our expectation and hope.

Rehearsal Notes

This script is for three readers. Readers should be encouraged to give heartfelt voice to the longing and expectation in these words. If they can embody these sentiments in the way they read, the audience will be drawn into the prayer.

The opening parenthetical comment which recurs throughout the reading is a verbal reminder of the shadowy context in which we wait. The high point of the reading occurs near the end with the words from Isaiah 9:6-7, the announcement of the child who is born. As the "titles" are declared, this section should crescendo and increase in tempo slightly, climaxing with "forevermore!" The tone of the reading drops again to more reflective waiting with the words "Watch, wait, be alert...."

Worship Planning

This reading works well on the first Sunday of Advent, as we begin the season of waiting. It could be used as the call to worship and followed with the hymn "Come, Thou Long-expected Jesus." Or it might serve as an introduction to prayer. The song "The Light Shines in the Darkness" (No. 9 in this book) could be used as a response to the prayer.

As a benediction, consider using the words of Isaiah 60:1-3 and singing the song "Arise, Shine" (No. 10 in this book).

The People Who Walk in Darkness

1	(...The people who walk in darkness ...
2	Those who dwell in a land of deep darkness ...)
3	Out of the depths we cry to you,
1	O Lord, hear our prayer!
3	Listen, O Lord,
2	listen
3	to the sound of our supplication.
1	If you would count sins, God, who could stand?
2	But there is forgiveness with you—
3	we stand in awe.
1	(... the people who walk in darkness ...
2	those who dwell in a land of deep darkness ...)
3	Out of the depths we cry to you!
1	O Lord, hear our prayer!
2	We wait for God!
3	The people wait!
2	And in God's Word we hope!
1	My soul waits for God, more than those who watch for the morning—
3	more than those who watch for the morning....
1	(... the people who walk in darkness ...
2	Those who dwell in a land of deep darkness ...)
1	Watch.
2	Wait.
3	Be alert!
2	For you do not know when the time will come!
1	Watch.
2	Wait.
3	Be alert!
1	For you do not know when the time will come!
3	O Israel, hope in God!
2	Wait for the Lord!
1	For with God there is steadfast love!
3	With God is salvation aplenty!

2	The people who walked in darkness have seen a great light.
1	Those who dwelt in the land of deep darkness, on them has light shined.

3	For to us a child is born, a son is given:
2	Wonderful Counselor,
1	Mighty God,
3	Everlasting Father,
2	Prince of Peace,
1	justice and righteousness,
3	increase and peace,
2	from this time forth,
3	forevermore!

1	Watch.
2	Wait.
3	Be alert!
2	For you do not know when the time will come.
1	Watch.
2	Wait.
3	Be alert!
1	For you do not know when the time will come.
2	(...The people who walk in darkness ...
1	Those who dwell in the land of deep darkness ...)
3	Out of the depths, we cry to you!
1,2,3,4	Lord, hear our prayer!

Adapted from Psalm 130; Isaiah 9:2, 6-7; and Mark 13:33.

27. Ancient Advent Songs

Background

The opening chapters of Matthew and Luke contain the ancient Advent songs of several biblical characters. In our preparations for Christmas, what are the Advent songs we sing as we await the coming of God's Messiah? the silent song of Joseph? the jubilant hymn of Mary? the skeptical chorus of Zechariah? or the responsive song of Elizabeth? Can we hear Gabriel's song, "Fear not, God is with you! God is bringing new birth!" This reading dramatizes these ancient Advent songs and invites us to ponder our hopes and expectations in the Advent season.

Rehearsal Notes

This script is for six readers: a narrator, Joseph, Zechariah, Gabriel, Elizabeth, and Mary. Each of the characters reflects on the circumstances and "sings" an Advent song. Readers should be encouraged to embody in their reading the silent resignation, anticipation, skepticism, or joy of their particular songs.

Worship Planning

This reading is intended for the first or second week of Advent. After the presentation of the ancient Advent songs, invite three or four persons to reflect for five minutes on their own individual Advent songs: What in particular are they waiting for, hoping for this Advent season? Introduce the reading with some opening words that incorporate elements of the background information given above, and encourage people to consider their own Advent songs and yearnings. You might conclude the opening words by reading stanza 3 of "O Little Town of Bethlehem."

Printing the following order of service will enable the congregation to follow the flow of the service.

Readers Theater	"Ancient Advent Songs" (adapted from Matthew and Luke)
	Opening Words
	Joseph's Song
	Gabriel's Song
	Zechariah's Song
Hymn	"Let All Mortal Flesh Keep Silence" (stanza 1)
	Elizabeth's Song
	Mary's Song
Hymn	"My Soul Proclaims with Wonder"
Our Advent Songs	Reflections
Hymn	"Come, Thou Long-expected Jesus"

If "My Soul Proclaims with Wonder" is unfamiliar, use "O Come, O Come, Immanuel."

Ancient Advent Songs

{To begin the reading, Zechariah, Joseph, the narrator, and Gabriel stand in that order. Elizabeth and Mary remain seated. As the narrator begins to speak, Joseph steps forward and stands silently.}

Narrator: When Mary had been betrothed to Joseph, before they came
together, she was found to be with child of the Holy Spirit.
And her husband, Joseph, being a just man and
unwilling to put her to shame, resolved to divorce her quietly.
But as he considered this, an angel of the Lord appeared
to him in a dream, saying:

Gabriel: Joseph, do not be afraid to take Mary, your wife,
for that which is conceived in her is of the Holy Spirit ...

Narrator: When Joseph woke from sleep, he did as the Lord
commanded him; he took Mary as his wife ...

Joseph: *{after a brief silence}*
I am always the last to know.
I must wait to hear in my dreams.
Do I interpret them correctly, or am I guessing?
My advent song is a silent song—
but my waiting is active ...
I awake and follow my dreams.

{Joseph steps back and Gabriel steps forward.}

Gabriel: Listen to Gabriel's Advent song!
Do not be afraid, Mary, for you have found favor with God!
Do not be afraid, Zechariah, for your prayer is answered!
Both of you shall know the birth of a child:
you will have joy and gladness!
The one child will be great, called the Son of the Most High!
And of his kingdom there will be no end!
The other child, John, will go before him
in the spirit and power of Elijah:
to turn the hearts of the parents to the children,
to turn the disobedient to the wisdom of the just,
to make ready for God a people prepared.

{an aside; more conversational tone}
Oh, do not fear my coming.
This really is good news!
See me as God's presence come to you!
It is a sign of your favor in God's eyes!
The Lord is with you! Stop the trembling!

God is moving among you, people,
with a power you cannot conceive!
Your questions are human questions;
with God, nothing is impossible.
{Gabriel steps back.}

{*Zechariah steps forward.*}

Narrator: Zechariah said to the angel:

Zechariah: How can I believe this?
I am an old man, and my wife is advanced in years!

Gabriel: Behold, you will be silent and unable to speak
until the day that these things come to pass,
because you did not believe my words
which will be fulfilled in their time.

{*more conversational, reflective*}

Zechariah: But how do I know? Could you give me a sign?
This doesn't make sense; we are both old!
Let's talk reason! It makes sense to be skeptical!

My questions are not answered: I am struck dumb!
Is this an answer to prayer?
Or a sign of my disobedience?

Oh, later, I will sing—when the child is born
and I see promise bear fruit in experience.
But for now, my Advent song leaves me speechless.
Skeptical—or awed??—and speechless ...

Narrator: And the people were waiting for Zechariah,
and they wondered at his delay in the temple.
And when Zechariah came out, he could not speak to them,
and they perceived that he had seen a vision in the temple.
And he made signs to them and remained dumb.

{*Readers return to seats as congregation sings stanza 1 of the hymn "Let All Mortal Flesh Keep Silence." After a brief silence, the narrator, Mary, and Elizabeth come forward.*}

Narrator: In those days, Mary arose and went with haste
into the hill country to a city of Judah.
And she entered the house of Zechariah and greeted Elizabeth.
And when Elizabeth heard the greeting of Mary,
the baby leaped in her womb!

Elizabeth: When I heard your voice, Mary,
I felt these stirrings deep within me!
I want to rejoice!!—for you, for me, for women, for your belief!
But more for God's faithfulness!
In bringing this new life we have waited for!
My Advent song comes in response to you!
Your belief is contagious!
And your acceptance has called forth hope in me—
and is a blessing to us both!

Mary: *{conversationally}*
The news was strange and my response predictable!
How can this be, since I have no husband?
This is unfathomable! Humanly strange!
But I am struck by God's possibility and open to the future.
Let it be according to God's Word.

This is an act of God's mercy;
it is empowering to all of us who feel unnoticed,
who disappoint ourselves.
I thought I would be overlooked.
But this is a promise fulfilled—
not to me, but to my people!
This is God's work among the lowly.
God will lift us up!

{in jubilant, songful voice}
My soul magnifies the Lord;
my spirit rejoices in you, God, my Savior!
For your regard has blessed me,
a poor woman of meager means,
From this day all generations will call me blessed!

For you, O Mighty One, have done great things for me!
Your name is Holy!
And your mercy is on those who fear you
from generation to generation.

You have shown strength with your arm.
You have scattered the proud in the imagination of their hearts.
You have put down the mighty from their thrones
and have lifted up the powerless.
You have filled the hungry with good things,
and have sent the rich away empty.
Remembering your mercy,
you have helped your people Israel—
as you promised Abraham and Sarah
mercy to their children forever!

Adapted from Matthew 1:18-20 and Luke 1 and 2 by Raylene Hinz-Penner and Patricia J. Shelly.

28. A Perceptive Story

Background

This reading dramatically portrays the healing of the man born blind in John 9. In this story, Jesus heals the physical blindness of one person and pronounces judgment on the spiritual blindness of people with healthy eyes.

As a "moral" to this story, the script presents Jesus' analogy of the eye as the lamp of the body (Matthew 6:22-23). Those who have eyes to see, let them see!

Rehearsal Notes

This script is designed for seven readers. You will need three strips of cloth for three blindfolds. Find cloth long enough to tie easily. (I have usually used white tea towels.)

The blindfolds are to visually contrast the physical blindness of the "blind man" with the spiritual "blindness" of the Pharisees. Rehearse the blindfolding sequence until it occurs smoothly and doesn't interrupt the flow of the story. "Pharisees" may have to memorize parts of their last lines. They stand silently blindfolded until the end of the reading.

The closing sentence is chanted rhythmically as a round by four of the readers. Note the instructions in the script and rehearse until readers feel comfortable with the timing and rhythm of this closing word.

Worship Planning

As a prelude to this reading, have the congregation sing the first stanza of "Amazing Grace!" Following the reading, use the ballad "John Nine" (No. 11 in this book). Other appropriate hymns for the service include "Be Thou My Vision" and "Awake, Awake, Fling Off the Night."

List the following in your bulletin so that the congregation can follow the flow of the reading:

A Perceptive Story (from John 9)
> Hymn Setting   "Amazing Grace" (stanza 1)
> Readers Theater "A Perceptive Story"
> Song   "John Nine"

A Perceptive Story

{Seven readers stand in a line facing the audience, the blind man (Reader 5) on one end, the Pharisees (Readers 6 and 7) on the other. Three strips of cloth are needed to use as blindfolds. The blind man wears a blindfold at first, then removes it when narrator says he can see. Readers 2 and 3 blindfold Pharisees at the point indicated in script, quickly and unobtrusively from behind. The Pharisees remain blindfolded for the remainder of the scene.}

1	As Jesus was walking along, he saw a man, blind from his birth. And the disciples questioned him:
2	Teacher, whose sin caused this man to be born blind?
3	Was it his sin? Or his parents' sin?
4	His blindness has nothing to do with his sins or his parents' sin. He is blind so that God's power might be seen at work in him. While daylight lasts, we must do the work of the one who sent me. Night is coming when no one can work. While I am in the world, I am the Light of the world.
1	Then Jesus spat on the ground and made some mud. He rubbed the mud on the man's eyes and said:
4	Go and wash your face in the pool at Siloam.
1	So the man went and washed his face. When he returned, he could see.
	{Reader 5 removes blindfold.}
2	Aren't we this man's neighbors?
3	Isn't he the one who used to sit and beg?
2	Yes, I think he's the one!
3	No, that isn't the man. It just looks like him!
5	It's me. I'm the man.
2	Then how were your eyes opened?
5	The man called Jesus—he made some mud, rubbed it on my eyes, and told me to wash my face in the pool at Siloam. So I went, and as soon as I washed, I could see.
3	Where is this man?
5	I don't know.

1   The neighbors took the man to the Pharisees.
(Now the day that Jesus cured the man of his blindness
was a Sabbath day.) And the Pharisees asked the man again
how he had gained his sight.

5   He put some mud on my eyes; then I washed and now I can see.

6   The man who did this cannot be from God,
for he does not obey the Sabbath law.

7   How could a man who is a sinner perform such miracles as this?

1   The Pharisees could not agree;
so they continued to question him:

6   You say he cured you of your blindness—
what do you say of him?

5   He is a prophet.

1   The Jewish authorities could not believe
that the man had been blind and could now see,
until they called his parents and asked them:

6   Is this your son?

7   You say that he was born blind—how is it, then, that he can see?

2   We know that he is our son.

3   And we know that he was born blind.

2   But we do not know how it is that he is now able to see.

3   Nor do we know who cured him of his blindness.

2   Ask him.

3   He is old enough.

2   Let him speak for himself.

1   His parents said this because they were afraid
of the Jewish leaders, who had already agreed
that anyone believing Jesus was the Messiah
should be banned from the synagogue.
A second time they called back the man who had been born blind.

6   Promise before God that you will tell the truth.

7   We know that the man who cured you is a sinner.

5   I do not know if he is a sinner or not.
One thing I do know: Once I was blind and now I can see.

6   What did he do to you? How did he cure you of your blindness?

5   I have already told you, and you would not listen!
Why do you want to hear it again?
Do you want to be his disciples, too?

7   Listen, you sinner, you are that fellow's disciple.
     We are disciples of Moses. We know that God spoke to Moses.
     As for that fellow, we do not even know where he comes from.

5   What a strange thing! You do not know where he comes from,
     but he cured me of blindness.
     We all know that God does not listen to sinners.
     But if anyone is a worshiper of God and does God's will,
     God listens to them! To open the eyes of someone born blind—
     that is a thing unheard of since the world began!
     Unless this man came from God, he would not be able to do this.

6   Who are you to give US lessons?

     {reader is blindfolded as he speaks}
7   You were born blind and brought up in sin. You can't teach us!
     Get out of the synagogue!

     {reader is blindfolded as he says last line}
6   Out.

1   Jesus heard that the blind man had been expelled from the
     synagogue, and he went to find the man.

4   Do you believe in the Son of Man?

5   Tell me who he is, sir, so that I can believe in him.

4   You have already seen him; he is the one talking to you.

5   I believe, Lord.

4   It is for judgment that I come into the world:
     that those who do not see may see,
     and that those who see may become blind.

     {speaking while blindfolded}
6,7 Are you saying we're blind?

4   If you were blind, you would be blameless,
     but since you claim to have sight, your guilt remains.

1   On another occasion, Jesus told this parable:

2   The eye is the lamp of the body.

3   If your eye is sound,

4   your whole body will be full of light.

5   If your eye is not sound,

2   your whole body will be full of darkness.

4   If the light in you is darkness, how great is the darkness!

{The following line is chanted rhythmically as a round by four readers. Each reader reads the whole sentence, beginning when the previous reader says the word "you" and emphasizing the word "great." Each slanted line represents a beat in the rhythm.}

         /   /   /   /   /   / /   / /

2   If the light in you is dark——ness, how GREAT is the dark-ness!

      3 If the light in you is   dark—-ness, how GREAT …

         4   If the light in you is dark—ness …

           5 If the light in you …

Adapted from John 9 and Matthew 6:22-23.

29. Ask, Seek, Knock

Background

While this reading begins and ends with the confident testimony of Psalm 46:1-3, the real focus is on Jesus' promise about asking and receiving (Matthew 7:7-8) and his counsel about anxiety and God's care (Matthew 6:25-33). This Psalm belongs with the Sermon on the Mount, for the message is the same: the God who is our refuge and strength will give us what we need.

Rehearsal Notes

This script is designed for four readers. The repetition is intended to assure people of God's pervasive provision. Encourage the readers to be expressive as they "exhort" the audience to believe the message of Scripture. The one line that all four readers say together should sound four times as loud! Rehearse this until it sounds confident and convincing.

You might try some simple gestures for the sequence "ask, seek, knock." Each person should develop a slightly different motion and use that gesture when saying "ask, seek, knock" as a single word.

Worship Planning

As a presentation of the Matthew texts, this reading is adaptable to many worship contexts. Depending on the specific theme of the service, it might be followed with one of these hymns:

> "Seek Ye First the Kingdom of God"
> "O God, in Restless Living"
> "Sometimes a Light Surprises"

Ask, Seek, Knock

1	God is.
2	God is.
3	God is our refuge.
4	God is our refuge and strength.
1	A very present help.
2	A very present help in time of trouble.
1,2,3,4	God is our refuge and strength.
3	Therefore we will not fear though the earth should change, though the mountains shake in the heart of the sea.
4	Therefore we will not fear though our lives should change, though our hearts shake with questions and doubts.
1	The God of hosts is with us.
2	The God of Jacob and Rachel is our refuge.
1	God is.
2	God is our refuge.
1,2,3,4	God is our refuge and strength.
1	Ask.
2	Seek.
3	Knock.
1	Ask.
2	Seek.
3	Knock.
1	Ask.
4	You shall receive.
2	Seek.
4	You shall find.
3	Knock.
4	It will be opened.
1	For everyone who asks, receives.
2	And the one who seeks, finds.
3	And to the one who knocks, it will be opened.

4	I tell you—do not be anxious about your life:
1	What shall we eat?
2	What shall we drink?
3	How will we pay for that?
1	Will we have enough?
2	What will the future be?
3	What shall we eat?
2	What shall we wear?
4	Do not be anxious for your life. God knows what you need and God will provide.
1	But seek first God's kingdom,
2	Seek God's reign in your life,
3	Seek first God's justice and righteousness, and you will have all you need.

1	Ask.
4	You shall receive.
2	Seek.
4	You shall find.
3	Knock.
4	It will be opened.
1	For everyone who asks, receives.
2	And the one who seeks, finds.
3	And to one who knocks, it will be opened.
1	Ask.
2	Seek.
3	Knock.
1	Ask.
2	Seek.
3	Knock.

1	God is.
2	God is.
3	God is our refuge.
4	God is our refuge and strength.
1	A very present help.
2	A very present help in time of trouble.
1,2,3,4	God is our refuge and strength.

3   Therefore we will not fear, though the earth should change,
     though the mountains shake in the heart of the sea.

4   Therefore we will not fear, though our lives should change,
     though our hearts shake with questions and doubts.

1   The God of hosts is with us.

2   The God of Jacob and Rachel is our refuge.

1   God is.

2   God is our refuge.

1,2,3,4   God is our refuge and strength.

Adapted from Psalm 46:1-3, 7 and Matthew 6:25-33; 7:7-8.

30. A Thanksgiving Reading

Background

Jesus cleanses ten lepers, but only one returns to give thanks (Luke 17:11-19). This reading is both a prayer of confession and a call to thanksgiving presented in the context of this story. The plea of the ten lepers ("Jesus, Master, have mercy on us") becomes the basis for our modern confession of sin and disease. The words of Psalm 103 are placed on the lips of the thankful leper, while Paul's instructions on prayer from Philippians 4 create a fitting introduction and conclusion.

Rehearsal Notes

This script for two readers moves from exhortation to storytelling and then back to exhortation. Readers should express these shifts in the tone of their voices. The story from Luke should be presented in a dramatic fashion, while the exhortation sections are a prayer for the whole congregation.

Worship Planning

This reading was originally created for a Thanksgiving service, but it can be adapted for a more general context. Open the service with a joyful call to praise and a hymn of thanksgiving (perhaps based on Psalm 103) and then use this readers theater script as an introduction to prayer, followed by a pastoral prayer.

A Thanksgiving Reading

2   In everything by prayer and supplication with thanksgiving,
let your requests be known to God.

1   "Jesus, Master, have mercy on us."

2   In our wickedness.

1   "Jesus, Master, have mercy on us."

2   In our sickness.

1   "Jesus, Master, have mercy on us."

2   In our selfishness.

1   As Jesus entered a village, he was met by ten lepers,
who stood at a distance and lifted up their voices and said,
"Jesus, Master, have mercy on us."

2   Have no anxiety about anything,
but in everything by prayer and supplication with thanksgiving
let your requests be made known to God.

1   "Jesus, Master, have mercy on us."
When Jesus saw the lepers, he said to them,

2   "Go show yourselves to the priests."

1   And as they went, they were cleansed.
Then one of them, a Samaritan, when he saw that he was healed,
turned back, praising God with a loud voice,
and fell on his face at Jesus' feet, giving thanks.
"Bless the Lord, O my soul, and all that is within me,
bless the holy name of God!
Bless the Lord, O my soul, and forget not all God's benefits:
who forgives all your iniquity, who heals all your diseases,
who redeems your life from the Pit,
who crowns you with steadfast love and mercy,
who satisfies you with good as long as you live,
so that your youth is renewed like the eagle's."

2   Then Jesus said, "Were not ten cleansed? Where are the nine?
Was no one found to return and give thanks to God except this foreigner?
Rise and go your way. Your faith has made you well."

1   Enter God's gates with thanksgiving, and God's courts with praise!

2   Give thanks and bless the name of God.

1   "Jesus, Master, have mercy on us."

2   We are driven to possess things.

1   "Jesus, Master, have mercy on us."

2	We are overfed.
1	"Jesus, Master, have mercy on us."
2	We make war on our enemies.
1	In everything by prayer and supplication with thanksgiving, let your requests be known to God.
2	Bless the Lord, O my soul.
1	"Jesus, Master, have mercy on us."

Adapted from Luke 17:11-19; Psalm 103:1-5; 100:4; and Philippians 4:6 by John McCabe-Juhnke and Patricia J. Shelly.

31. "Who Am I?" The Suffering One, The Transfigured One

Background

In Mark's Gospel, Jesus' first pronouncement that he must suffer and die is immediately followed by his glorious transfiguration. The disciples are forced to consider Jesus' question "Who do you say that I am?" in the contrast of these two moments. This short reading accentuates that contrast for the audience, particularly if it is followed by the singing of the two hymns listed in the worship notes.

Rehearsal Notes

This script is for four readers. Encourage the readers to "paint the scene" for the audience by the way they read. The brief pause is intended to highlight the contrast in the two scenes between Christ, the suffering one, and Christ, the transfigured one.

Worship Planning

I created this reading for use on one of the Sundays of Lent to provoke reflection on the identity of Christ as Passion Week approaches.

After the reading, the congregation should sing two hymns that contrast the images of Christ presented. Have the chorister or organist lead the transfiguration hymn with buoyant enthusiasm, and then lead the suffering hymn with more sober reflection. The leader will not have to explain what is happening; the experience of singing these two hymns back-to-back will be a powerful prelude to a time of silence and prayer. Print the following order in the bulletin, so that the congregation can follow the flow of the service:

> Readers Theater from Mark 8 and 9
> "Who Am I?" The Suffering One, The Transfigured One"
> Hymn of Transfiguration "All Hail the Power of Jesus' Name"
> Hymn of Suffering "When I Survey the Wondrous Cross"
> Time of Silence and Prayer

"Who Am I?" The Suffering One, The Transfigured One

1	And Jesus went on with his disciples to the villages of Caesarea Philippi; and on the way, he asked them,
2	Who do people say that I am?
3	John the Baptist,
4	others say Elijah,
3	or one of the prophets.
2	But who do you say that I am?
4	You are the Christ.
1	And he began to teach them that the Son of Man must suffer many things, and be rejected by the elders, the chief priests, and the scribes, and after three days rise again. He said this plainly.
4	God forbid, Lord! This shall never happen to you!
2	Get behind me, Satan! For you are not on the side of God but on the side of the world.
	{pause}
1	After six days, Jesus took with him Peter and James and John, and led them up on a high mountain apart by themselves.
3	And he was transfigured before them: his face shone like the sun, and his garments became white as light.
1	And there appeared to them Elijah and Moses; and they were talking with Jesus.
4	Master, it is well that we are here! Let us make three booths, one for you and one for Moses and one for Elijah!
1	And a cloud overshadowed them, and a voice came out of the cloud,
2	This is my beloved Son; listen to him.
4	And suddenly, looking around, they no longer saw anyone with them but Jesus only.

Adapted from Mark 8:27-33 and Mark 9:2-8.

32. Christ as King and Christ as Servant

Background

By contrasting the Palm Sunday story with the simple account of Jesus washing his disciples' feet, this reading presents the dual images of Christ as king and Christ as servant. While the Gospels convey this contrast in the telling of the Passion Week events, Philippians 2:6-11 portrays the same themes in song: the One who took the form of a servant has now been exalted and enthroned by God. This reading presents narratively the poetry of the Philippian hymn.

Rehearsal Notes

In this script, the four readers should convey the contrast in tone between the two images of Christ: the first scene is animated and enthusiastic; the second, sober and subdued.

Note the instructions given in the script for the Palm Sunday acclamations. The intention is to simulate a crowd—with four people! These lines should be rehearsed until readers are comfortable with the cadence and flow.

Rehearse the lines with multiple voices, so the readers are comfortable reading together. The goal is to add strength and tone to these lines by adding voices.

Worship Planning

This reading could be used on Palm Sunday or another Sunday of Lent. The point is to contrast the images of Jesus as king and servant. Print the following in the bulletin, so that the congregation can follow the flow of the comparison.

Reflection on Christ as King and Christ as Servant

	Readers Theater from the Gospel accounts of Palm Sunday
	"Christ as King and Christ as Servant"
Hymn	"All Hail the Power of Jesus' Name
Hymn	"Will You Let Me Be Your Servant?"

You might also incorporate into your service the song "Philippian Hymn" (No. 2 in this book), which juxtaposes the servant and royal images of Christ.

Christ as King and Christ as Servant

{Tone of the reading is excited and joyful.}

1	As Jesus was coming to Jerusalem,
2	as he drew near at the descent of the Mount of Olives,
1	the whole multitude of the disciples began to rejoice and praise God with a loud voice
1,2	for all the mighty works that they had seen:

3	Blessed is the King who comes in the name of the Lord!
4	Peace in heaven and glory in the highest!

{In the following lines, Reader 4 shouts "Hosanna" when reader 2 is saying "King" and "Lord"; Reader 3 shouts "Hallelujah" when reader 1 is saying "God" and "highest."}

2   Blessed is the King who comes in the name of the Lord!

              4 Hosanna!   4 Hosanna!

1   Glory to God, to God in the highest!

              3 Hallelujah!   3 Hallelujah!

2	They took branches and went out to meet him:
3	Hosanna to the King of Israel!
1	And Jesus found a donkey and sat upon it.
2	For the prophet Zechariah said:
4	Fear not, daughter of Zion! Your King is coming! Riding on a donkey!

1	And many spread their garments on the road,
2	and others spread leafy branches they had cut from the field.

1	And those who went before and those who went after cried out:
3	Blessed is the kingdom of our father David that is coming!
4	Hosanna!
3	Hosanna!
3,4	Hosanna in the highest!

2	Teacher, rebuke your disciples!
1	Do you hear what they are saying!
2	Rebuke your disciples!

3   I tell you, if these were silent, the very stones would cry out!

4   (If these were silent, the very stones would cry out!)

         {Read as before.}

2   Blessed is the King who comes in the name of the Lord!

                    4 Hosanna!   4 Hosanna!

1   Glory to God, to God in the highest!

                 3 Hallelujah!   3 Hallelujah!

{Readers sit down as congregation sings "All Hail the Power of Jesus' Name" and return when the hymn is finished.}

         {Tone is quiet, reflective.}

1   Jesus rose from supper, laid aside his garments,
         and girded himself with a towel.

2   He poured water into a basin and began to wash the disciples'
         feet and to wipe them with the towel he had around his waist.

3   Lord, do you wash my feet?

4   You shall never wash my feet!

1   What I am doing, you will only understand later.
         If I do not wash you, you will not be a part of me.

2   When he had washed their feet, he replaced his garments
         and resumed his place.

1   Do you know what I have done to you?

2   You call me Teacher and King and Lord!

3   If I, then, your Teacher and Lord, have washed your feet,

4   you ought to wash one another's feet.

1   I have given you the example!

2   For whoever would be great among you must be your servant,

3   and whoever would be first among you must be slave of all.

4   For the Son of Man also came not to be served, but to serve,
         and to give his life as a ransom for many.

1   I have given you the example!

2   Let the greatest among you become as the youngest,

3   and the leader as one who serves.

1,2,3,4   For I am among you as One who serves!

{Readers sit down as congregation sings "Will You Let Me Be Your Servant?"}

Adapted from the Palm Sunday accounts in Luke 19:37-40; Matthew 21:5-9; and Mark 11:9-10—and John 13:4-16; Mark 10:42-45; and Luke 22:26-27.

33. The Spirit of God (Reading 1)

Background

This reading gathers up Scripture references concerning the Spirit of God from Genesis to the Gospel of John. These texts elaborate the movement of the Spirit in the world: hovering over the waters, creating and sustaining the world, pouring out on all flesh, comforting and befriending. The message is that God is powerfully and pervasively present to us.

Rehearsal Notes

This is a script for four readers. Since the reading intends to highlight the Spirit of God, readers should give a slight emphasis to these words when they appear in the script. Rehearse the unison lines so readers are comfortable with their rhythm and flow; the point of multiple voices is to increase volume and emphasis. Encourage readers to read with enthusiasm and expression.

Worship Planning

This reading was written as the first of a two-part reflection on the Spirit of God (see the next script), but it can also be used alone as a call to worship. If it is used as a call to worship, follow it with a hymn like "Holy Spirit, Come with Power" or another hymn that invites the presence of the Spirit into the midst of the congregation.

To use as a two-part sequence, see the worship notes on the next reading.

There are many hymns with vivid, evocative images of the Spirit; check the topical index in any hymnal under "Holy Spirit."

The Spirit of God (Reading 1)

1 In the beginning, when God created the heavens and the earth,
   the earth was formless, chaos, darkness, confusion.

2 And the SPIRIT OF GOD was hovering over the face of the waters.

3 O God, the earth is full of your creatures;
   in wisdom you have made them all.

4 You send forth your SPIRIT and they are created.
   You renew the face of the earth.

3 God says, "I will pour out my SPIRIT on all flesh,
   your sons and daughters shall prophesy;

2 your old people will dream dreams;
   and your young people will see visions.

4 Even on servants and slaves, in those days,
   I will pour out my SPIRIT."

2 Hovering over the waters,

3 pouring out on all flesh,

1 creating,

4 sustaining ...

1,2,3,4 Come! Know the presence of God!

4 Jesus said, "I will ask the Father,
   and God will give you another Counselor to be with you forever—
   even the SPIRIT OF TRUTH.

2 The Counselor, the SPIRIT OF TRUTH,
   whom God will send in my name,
   will teach you all things and remind you of all I have said.

1 I have yet many things to say to you, but you cannot bear them now.
   But the SPIRIT OF TRUTH will come and guide you into all truth."

3 And on the evening of the first day of the week ...
   Jesus came and stood among them and said,

2 "Peace be with you. As the Father has sent me, so I send you."

1 And when he had said this, he breathed on them and said,
   "Receive the HOLY SPIRIT."

2 Hovering over the waters,

3 pouring out on all flesh,

1 as close as your next breath,

4 comforting, befriending.

1,2,3,4 Come! Know the presence of God!

Adapted from Genesis 1:1-2; Psalm 104:24, 30; Joel 2:28-29; and John 14:17, 26; 16:12-13; 20:19-20.

34. The Spirit of God (Reading 2)

Background

While the previous script draws on texts from Genesis to John, this reading uses a wealth of references in the New Testament for reflection on the Spirit of God. In addition to portions of Luke, Acts, John, Romans, and Revelation, this reading includes lines from the song "Veni Sancte Spiritus" as it invites us to "Come, know the presence of God."

Rehearsal Notes

This script is for four readers. Since the reading seeks to highlight the Spirit of God, readers should give a slight emphasis to these words when they appear in the script.

Rehearse the lines with multiple voices until readers are comfortable with their rhythm and flow. The point of adding voices is to increase volume and emphasis. Near the end of the reading is a sentence where voices are added as the first reader continues to speak. Here the first reader is the leader, and the others should join, matching that person's rhythm and tone so the sentence will crescendo to the end. Encourage readers to read with enthusiasm and expression.

Worship Planning

This reading was created as the second part of a two-part reflection on the Spirit of God (see preceding script), but it may also be used alone as a call to worship or a call to prayer (see notes for previous script). Most hymnals include many hymns with vivid, evocative images of the Spirit; check the topical index under "Holy Spirit."

This reading, along with "Spirit of God (Reading 1)," was created for a service whose theme was "Images of the Spirit of God." Print the following order in the bulletin so the congregation can follow the flow of the presentation:

Reflections on the Spirit of God	
Hymn	"Come, O Creator Spirit, Come" (stanzas 1,4)
Readers Theater	"Spirit of God (Reading 1)"
Hymn	"God Sends Us the Spirit"
Readers Theater	"Spirit of God (Reading 2)"
Hymn	"Veni Sancte Spiritu"

In such a service, you might use a call to worship and benediction that focus also on the Spirit of God. Consider "Gracious Spirit, Dwell with Me" as a closing hymn.

Spirit of God (Reading 2)

1   God is SPIRIT, and those who worship God
    must worship in spirit and in truth.

2   Now when Jesus had been baptized and was praying,
    the heaven was opened, and the HOLY SPIRIT
    descended upon him like a dove.

3   On the day of Pentecost, the disciples were all together
    in one place, and suddenly a sound came from heaven
    like the rush of a mighty wind,

4   and there appeared to them tongues as of fire ...
    and they were filled with the HOLY SPIRIT.

3   The SPIRIT is like the wind:
    the wind blows where it wills, you hear the sound of it,
    but you do not know where it is coming from,
    or where it is going.

2   The SPIRIT is like water:
    for those who receive the Holy Spirit—
    out of their hearts shall flow rivers of living water!

1   And the SPIRIT helps us in our weakness,
    for we do not know how to pray as we should,
    but the Spirit intercedes for us
    with sighs too deep for words.

4   The Spirit and the Bride say,

3   "Come!"

4   Let those who hear say,

1,2,3 "Come!"

2   Let the thirsty take the water of life without price.

1   Come, Holy Spirit!

3   Come!

2   From heaven shine forth with your light!

1   Come from the four winds! Come, breath of God!

4   Disperse the shadows over us;
    renew and strengthen your people.

3   You are only comforter, peace of the soul.

2   In the heat, you shade us;
    in our labor, you refresh us;

4   and in times of trouble, you are our strength.

1	Come, Holy Spirit,
1,2	and kindle in our hearts the flame of your love
1,2,3	that in the darkness of the world, it may glow
1,2,3,4	and reach to all, forever!
1	And the Spirit of God is hovering on the waters ...
3	blowing like the wind ...
2	flowing like living waters ...
4	descending like a dove, alighting like tongues of fire ...
1	pouring out on all flesh,
2	groaning with sighs too deep for words.
1	Creating, enlightening,
2	comforting, befriending.
1,2,3,4	Come! Know the presence of God!

Adapted from John 4:24; Luke 3:21-22; Acts 2:1-4; John 3:8; 8:38-39; Romans 8:28; Revelation 22:17; and lines from the song "Veni Sancte Spiritu" (Copyright © 1978, 80, 81 by Les Presses de Taize [France]. Used by permission of GIA Publications Inc., exclusive agent. All rights reserved).

35. With Thanksgiving

Background

This reading elaborates Paul's instructions about prayer in Philippians 4:6 by exploring the themes of thanksgiving, anxiety, supplication, and God's generous provision. In doing so, it incorporates some of Jesus' teachings from the Sermon on the Mount and calls us to pray "with thanksgiving."

Rehearsal Notes

This script for two readers is instruction on prayer, so it should be read with a tone of earnestness and encouragement. Invite the readers to emphasize the words "with thanksgiving" which recur throughout the script.

Worship Planning

This reading was originally created for a Thanksgiving service, to be followed with any Thanksgiving hymn ("Sing to the Lord of Harvest" or "For the Fruit of All Creation"). But it could be used more generally as a call to prayer or thanksgiving and followed with a prayer hymn (like "Lord, Listen to Your Children") or a Thanksgiving hymn (like "When All Thy Mercies, O My God").

With Thanksgiving

1	Have no anxiety about anything,
2	but in everything, by prayer and supplication
1	WITH THANKSGIVING,
2	let your requests be made known to God.

1	Ask—it will be given you. Seek—you will find. Knock—it will be opened to you. For everyone who asks, receives, the one who seeks, finds, to the one who knocks, it will be opened.

2	Have no anxiety about anything,
1	but in everything, by prayer and supplication
2	WITH THANKSGIVING,
1	let your requests be made known to God.

2	Therefore do not be anxious, saying, "What shall we eat?" "What shall we wear?" God knows that you need these things. But seek first God's kingdom and righteousness, and you will have all you need.

1	Have no anxiety about anything, but in everything, by prayer and supplication WITH THANKSGIVING,
2	let your requests be made known to God.

1	I do not complain of want. For I have learned to be content with whatever I have. I know what it is to have little, and I know what it is to have plenty. In any and all circumstances, I have learned the secret of facing plenty and hunger, abundance and want. I can do all things through the One who strengthens me. For God will supply every need according to his riches in glory in Christ Jesus.

2   Blessed are the poor in spirit,
    for theirs is the kingdom of heaven.
    Blessed are those who hunger and thirst for righteousness;
    they shall be satisfied.
    Blessed are the peacemakers,
    for they shall be called children of God.

1   In everything, by prayer and supplication

2   WITH THANKSGIVING,

1   let your requests be made known to God.

2   And the peace of God which passes all understanding

1   will keep your hearts and minds in Christ Jesus.

Adapted from Philippians 4:6, 11-13, 19 and Matthew 5:3, 6, 9; 6:31-33; 7:7-8.

Readings from Paul

36. Parable of the Body
37. Present Your Bodies a Living Sacrifice
38. Christ Is Our Peace (Reading 1)
39. Christ Is Our Peace (Reading 2)
40. Ministry of Reconciliation
41. The Breadth and Length and Height and Depth
42. Awake, Rise, and Christ Will Shine on You

36. Parable of the Body

Background

This reading dramatizes Paul's illustration of the variety of gifts in 1 Corinthians 12. It may be a stretch to call it a parable, but the script adopts a narrative style and humor to illustrate Paul's teaching that we all have a place in the body of Christ. Paul also uses the body metaphor in Ephesians 5 which provides a fitting end to the exhortation.

Rehearsal Notes

This parable is written for five readers. The "heart" sits on a chair, while the other four readers gather around in a way that visually suggests a body. The "hand" and the "foot" could sit or kneel in front of the chair.

Encourage each "body part" to verbalize its jealousy or disdain with dramatic expression. The "heart" interrupts to call all the body parts back to a unified identity. The ending of the reading should increase in tempo and volume.

In the last sentence, one person begins reading and other voices are added as the sentence builds to an enthusiastic climax. The first person should act as leader, reading the whole sentence in a normal cadence. The added voices join, matching the first reader's pace and phrasing. Practice the unison lines until readers are comfortable reading together.

Worship Planning

A service focused on "many gifts" or "the body of Christ" could also include a reading of other parts of 1 Corinthians 12. Using the readers theater provides variety in the presentation of this chapter. One could read verses 1-11, do the parable dramatization, then conclude with a reading of verses 27-30.

The song "Many Gifts" (No. 12 in this book) could be used as a congregational response, both re-enforcing and celebrating the scriptural insight. Also, using "Love Song" (No. 13 in this book) would extend consideration to 1 Corinthians 13.

The Parable of the Body

{Staging for five readers: Reader 5 (the heart) sits in a chair with Readers 1 and 4 (eye and ear) standing side by side behind the chair and Readers 2 and 3 (hand and foot) standing on either side of the chair. The idea is to visually suggest a body by the way the readers stand together.}

	{proclaiming}
1,2	Hear the word of the Lord!
1	For just as the body is one and has many members,
2	and all the members together form one body—
3,4	so it is with Christ!

3	For by one Spirit, we were all baptized into one body:
4	male or female,
1	Jew or Greek,
2	slave or free.
4	And the body does not consist of one member, but of many!

	{More dramatically}
1	If the foot were to say:
2	I'm not a hand; I'm not a part of the body; I wish I were a hand!
3	Or if the ear would say:
4	I'm not an eye; I wish I were an eye; I'm not a part of the body!
1	That would not make it any less a part of the body.
3	As it is, the body has many parts, and all belong to one body!
2	So the eye cannot say:
1	Hand, I don't need you. You might as well leave!

4	And the hand cannot say:
3	I don't need you at all, feet; I get along fine without you!
	{interrupting}
5	Wait a minute!
	{surprised}
1,2,3,4	Who's that?
5	This is the heart! Hand, where would you be without the feet to carry you around? And foot, what would you do without the hand to help you put on your shoes? And ear, how dull the world would be if you didn't have the eye to help you see!

{with dawning recognition}

4	We need each other!
3	We have to work together!
1	We are to grow up in every way into Christ,
2	who is the head of the Body.
3	And when we work together,
3,4	and take care of each other,
2,3,4,5	we grow together.
1,2,3,4	And upbuild ourselves in love!

Adapted from 1 Corinthians 12:12-26 and Ephesians 5:15-16.

Let All Within Us Praise! Dramatic Resources for Worship by Patricia J. Shelly, copyright © 1996 by Faith & Life Press. Permission is granted to photocopy this script for use in practice and performance.

37. Present Your Bodies a Living Sacrifice

Background

This reading connects Paul's exhortation in Romans 12:1-2 with his teaching in Colossians 3:9-17. What does it mean to be "transformed by the renewal of your minds?" A detailed response occurs in Colossians where Paul instructs us to put off the "old self" and describes the qualities of the "new self" we should put on. Finally, he urges us to let the "peace of Christ rule" in our hearts.

Rehearsal Notes

Encourage the two readers to speak with sincerity and earnestness. They are exhorting their "brothers and sisters" and encouraging them to grow spiritually. Rehearse the unison lines until readers can speak together with expression and ease.

Worship Planning

This reading will work well in presenting the Romans 12:1-2 or Colossians 3:9-17 texts as the focus of a service. Consider using the song "Philippian Hymn" (No. 2 in this book) or the hymn "Create My Soul Anew" as a response to the reading.

Present Your Bodies a Living Sacrifice

{with strong voice}

1,2   Brothers and sisters,

2   by the mercies of God, present your bodies
as a living sacrifice, holy and acceptable to God:

1   a living sacrifice, the worship offered by mind and heart.[7]

2   Do not be conformed to the pattern of this world,

1   but be transformed by the renewal of your minds,
so that you may discern the will of God—

2   what is good, acceptable, and perfect.

1   You have put off the old self with all its practices
and have clothed yourselves with the new self,

2   which is being constantly renewed in the image of its Creator.

1   So put on the garments that suit God's people:
compassion, kindness, lowliness, meekness, and patience,

2   forbearing one another, and, if one has a complaint against another,
forgiving each other, as the Lord has forgiven you.

1   And above all these, put on love

1,2   which binds everything together in perfect harmony.

1   Let the peace of Christ rule in your hearts
to which you were called in one body.

2   And be thankful.

1   And whatever you do in word or deed,
do everything in the name of the Lord Jesus,

2   giving thanks to God the Father through him.

1,2   Brothers and sisters,

2   by the mercies of God, present your bodies
as a living sacrifice, holy and acceptable to God:

1   a living sacrifice, the worship offered by heart and mind.

2   Do not be conformed to the pattern of this world,

1   but be transformed by the renewal of your minds,
so that you may discern the will of God—

2   what is good, acceptable, and perfect.

[7]New English Bible. Oxford: Oxford University Press, 1970.

Adapted from Romans 12:1-2 and Colossians 3:9-10, 12-17.

38. Christ Is Our Peace (Reading 1)

Background

This reading and the following one present an interpretation of Ephesians 2:11-19. In this setting, Christ's work on the cross is presented as the "new thing" God is doing in the world, by invoking Isaiah 43:10 and Revelation 21:5. In addition, Jesus' rendition of Isaiah 61 is quoted as a way of describing the "peace" that Christ announced with his earthly ministry.

Rehearsal Notes

Encourage the four readers to speak the opening announcement (which is repeated at the end) with exuberance and joy. Practice the unison line ("I make all things new!") until all are comfortable reading together.

The Ephesians text should also have the tone of an exhortation. On the first page, as three of the readers explain how "Christ is our peace," a fourth reader repeats these words several times. This repetition should have a steady insistence, almost as a "beating" tone underneath the explication. This whole section should build in intensity through the line "thereby bringing hostility to an end." After a brief pause, the reading begins again at a lower "plateau" and builds in intensity to the end.

Worship Planning

This reading may be used when Ephesians 2:11-19 is the Scripture text chosen for a worship service. Consider using one of the following hymns or songs as an introduction or response to the Scripture:

> "O Praise the Gracious Power"
> "Prayer for Peace" (No. 3 in this book)
> "In Christ There Is No East or West"
> "For We Are Strangers No More"
> "We Are People of God's Peace"

Christ Is Our Peace (Reading 1)

1	Behold!
2	Behold!
3	I am doing a new thing!
4	Now it springs forth—don't you see it?
1	Behold!
2	Behold!
1,2,3,4.	I make all things new!
3	Remember.
4	Remember,
3	that you were at one time separated from Christ,
2	alienated from the people of God,
1	strangers to the covenants of promise,
4	having no hope,
3	and without God in the world.
4	But now in Christ Jesus, you who once were far off have been brought near.
1	For Christ is our peace,
2	(Christ is our peace.)
4	who has made us both one,
2	(Christ is our peace.)
3	and has broken down the dividing wall of hostility
2	(Christ is our peace.)
1	that he might create in himself one new person
2	(Christ is our peace.)
3	in place of two, thus making peace.
2	(Christ is our peace.)
4	And reconciling us to God in one body through the cross,
2	(Christ is our peace.)
3	thereby bringing hostility to an end.
	{pause before going on}
1	And Christ came and preached peace to you who were far off and peace to you who were near.
2	For through him we both have access in one Spirit to God.

3	So then, you are no longer strangers and sojourners,
4	no longer "we" and "they,"
2	no longer Jew or Greek,
1	no longer "insider" and "outsider,"
3	but you are fellow citizens with the saints and members of the household of God.
4	You are no longer children tossed to and fro and carried about with every wind of doctrine by human cunning,
1	but you are members of the body of Christ.
2	And Christ is our peace.
1	The Spirit of the Lord is upon me,
2	because God has anointed me to preach good news to the poor.
3	God has sent me to proclaim release to the captives, recovery of sight to the blind,
4	to set at liberty those who are oppressed.
2	to proclaim—
3	to proclaim—
1	Behold!
2	Behold!
3	I am doing a new thing!
4	Now it springs forth—don't you see it?
1	Behold!
2	Behold!
1,2,3,4	Christ is our peace!

Adapted from Isaiah 43:10; Revelation 21:5; Ephesians 2:11-19; 4:14; and Luke 4:18-19.

39. Christ Is Our Peace (Reading 2)

Background

This reading and the preceding one present an interpretation of Ephesians 2:11-19. This rendition uses Paul's exclamation in Romans 11:33 as the frame for his description of God's work in Christ. In addition, it incorporates elements of Paul's earlier comments in Ephesians 2:4-8 where God's grace is connected to the peace God makes for us in Christ Jesus.

Rehearsal Notes

This script is written for four readers. Encourage the readers to speak with exuberance and joy, as if speaking these words for the first time. This reading should have the tone of an exhortation. Rehearse the one unison line so that it can be read with ease.

Worship Planning

This reading may be used when Ephesians 2:11-19 is the Scripture text chosen for a worship service. Consider using one of the following hymns or songs as an introduction or response to the Scripture:

> "O Praise the Gracious Power"
> "Prayer for Peace" (No. 3 in this book)
> "For We are Strangers No More"
> "What Mercy and Divine Compassion"
> "Great God of Wonders"

Christ Is Our Peace (Reading 2)

1	O the depth of the riches and wisdom and knowledge and grace of God!
2	How unsearchable are God's judgments!
3	How inscrutable God's ways!
4	Remember that you Gentiles were at one time separated from Christ,
2	alienated from the people of God,
1	strangers to the covenants of promise,
4	having no hope,
3	and without God in the world.
2	But now in Christ Jesus, you who once were far off have been brought near.
1	For Christ is our peace, who has made us both one,
3	and has broken down the dividing wall of hostility between us,
2	that he might create in himself one new humanity in place of two, thus making peace,
4	and reconciling us to God in one body through the cross, thereby bringing hostility to an end.
1	And Christ came and preached peace to you who were far off and peace to you who were near.
2	For through him we both have access in one Spirit to God.
3	So then, you are no longer strangers and sojourners,
2	no longer Jew or Greek,
1	no longer "insider" and "outsider,"
4	no longer "we" and "they,"
3	but you are fellow citizens with the saints and members of the household of God.
4	You are no longer children tossed to and fro and carried about with every wind of doctrine by human cunning,
1	but you are members of the body of Christ.
4	God, who is rich in mercy—
2	out of the great love with which God loved us—
4	made us alive together with Christ.
3	By grace you have been saved.
1,2,3,4	Abide in God's grace.
1	O the depth of the riches and wisdom and knowledge and grace of God!
2	How unsearchable are God's judgments!
3	How inscrutable God's ways!

Adapted from Ephesians 2:4-8, 11-22; 4:14; and Romans 11:33.

40. Ministry of Reconciliation

Background

This reading is a call to the ministry of reconciliation—an announcement that we are Christ's ambassadors in the world (2 Corinthians 5:17-20).

This call is grounded in the example of Christ ("I am among you as one who serves," Luke 22:24-27) and the appeal of Christ to his disciples ("Ask the Lord of the harvest to send out laborers," Matthew 9:35-38). Christ's ambassadors look forward to God's healing of the nations (Revelation 22:1-2) and God's renewal of the world (Revelation 21:1-4). It is this vision that sustains our labor.

Rehearsal Notes

In this script for four readers, the recurring exhortation ("that is, in Christ, God was reconciling ...") is interspersed with narrative reports from Christ's teaching ministry and John's vision in Revelation. Encourage readers to speak with dramatic emphasis and energy as they strive to make this word come alive for the audience.

Worship Planning

This reading may be used when 2 Corinthians 5:17-20 is the Scripture text chosen for a worship service, or when "missions" is the theme. Consider using one of the following hymns or songs as an introduction or response to the Scripture:

> "Prayer for Peace" (No. 3 in this book)
> "For the Healing of the Nations"
> "The Work is Thine, O Christ"
> "Lord, Whose Love in Humble Service"
> "Lord of Light, Your Name Outshining"

Ministry of Reconciliation

1 Therefore, if anyone is in Christ, there is a new creation.

2 The old has passed away. Behold the new has come.

3 All this is from God who, through Christ, reconciled us to God's self

4 and gave to us the ministry of reconciliation.

3 That is, in Christ, God was reconciling the world to God's self—

2 not counting their sins against them—

4 and entrusting to us the message of reconciliation.

1 So we are ambassadors for Christ, God making appeal through us.

3 And Jesus went about all the cities and villages,
teaching in their synagogues,

2 proclaiming the good news of the kingdom,
and curing every disease and sickness.

1 When he saw the crowds, he had compassion for them,
because they were harassed and helpless,

4 like sheep without a shepherd.

3 And he said to his disciples,

4 "The harvest is plentiful, but laborers are few.
Therefore, ask the Lord of the harvest
to send out laborers into his harvest."

1 That is, in Christ, God was reconciling the world to God's self—

2 and entrusting to us the ministry of reconciliation.

3 So we are ambassadors for Christ,

4 God making appeal through us!

2 A dispute also arose among them,
which of them was to be regarded as the greatest.
And Jesus said,

4 "The kings of the Gentiles lord it over them;
and those in authority over them are called benefactors.
But not so with you.

3 Rather, the greatest among you must become like the youngest,

1 and the leader like one who serves.

2 For who is greater, the one who is at the table
or the one who serves? Is it not the one at the table?

4 But I am among you as one who serves."

1	That is, in Christ, God was reconciling the world to God's self—
2	and entrusting to us the ministry of reconciliation.
3	So we are ambassadors for Christ,
4	God making appeal through us!

2	Then I saw a new heaven and a new earth,
3	for the first heaven and the first earth had passed away ...
4	And I saw the holy city, new Jerusalem, coming down out of heaven from God. And I heard a voice from the throne saying,
1	"See the home of God is among mortals! God will dwell with them as their God and they will be God's people....
2	God will wipe every tear from their eyes.
3	Death will be no more;
4	mourning and crying and pain will be no more.
1	For the first things have passed away."
2	Then the angel showed me the river of the water of life, bright as crystal, flowing from the throne of God and of the Lamb through the middle of the street of the city;
4	and the tree of life with its twelve kinds of fruit, on either side of the river ...
1	and the leaves of the tree are for the healing of the nations.

3	That is, in Christ, God was reconciling the world to God's self—
2	and entrusting to us the ministry of reconciliation.
4	So we are ambassadors for Christ,
1	God making appeal through us!
1,2,3,4	Ambassadors for Christ.
1	God making appeal through us!

Adapted from 2 Corinthians 5:17-20; Luke 22:24-27; Matthew 9:35-38; and Revelation 21:1-4; 22:1-2.

41. The Breadth and Length and Height and Depth

Background

The focus of this reading is a presentation of the Ephesians 3:17-19 text, enriched with insights from Psalm 139 and Romans 8. Both of the secondary texts explore the extent of God's presence and love in geographical and theological terms and so help us to comprehend the breadth and length and height and depth of God's love.

Rehearsal Notes

Encourage the four participants to read with enthusiasm and presence; the challenge is to make the Scripture come alive for the congregation.

Three times in this script, the readers "add voices" as they read. At these times, readers may be tempted to speak more softly and even to slow down; but the purpose of adding voices is to express "expansiveness" both in volume and texture. Have the first reader be the "leader" and read the whole phrase normally; it is up to the other readers to join the first at the appropriate time. Rehearse these sections until all four readers are comfortable with the cadence of the phrase.

Worship Planning

This reading emphasizes both the incomprehensible mystery of God's presence as well as the unsurpassable love of God's nature. Hymns that could be used as a response to such a reading include:

> "Love the Lord (With All)" (No. 1 in this book)
> "O Power of Love"
> "Love Divine, All Loves Excelling"
> "O Love That Will Not Let Me Go"

The Breadth and Length and Height and Depth

1   For this reason I bow my knees before the Father,
         from whom every family in heaven and on earth takes its name.

2   I pray that, according to the riches of God's glory,
         you may be strengthened in your inner being
         with power through his Spirit,

3   and that Christ may dwell in your hearts through faith,
         as you are being rooted and grounded in love.

4   I pray that you may have the power to comprehend, with all the saints,
         what is the breadth and length and height and depth ...

4   the breadth,

4,3   and length,

4,3,2   and height,

4,3,2,1   and depth!

1   Lord, you have searched me and known me!

2   You know if I am standing or sitting,

3   you perceive my thoughts from afar.

4   You have traced my journey and my resting places.

2   You are familiar with all my ways.

1   Lord, you have searched me and known me!

3   Before a word is on my tongue, you know it completely.

4   Close behind and close in front—you surround me,

3   sheltering me with your hand.

2   Such knowledge is beyond my understanding,

1   unsearchable, beyond my reach.

4   Where can I go to escape your Spirit?

1   What if I would try to flee from your presence?

3   If I climb to the heavens, you are there.

2   If I sink to the depths, you are there too!

1   If I fly to the point of the sunrise—

2   or far across the sea—

1   your hand would still be guiding me,

2   your right hand holding me.

2	If I asked darkness to cover me:
3	"Let there be night instead of light!"
2	Even darkness is not dark to you.
1	Night would shine as day for you.
4	Such knowledge is too wonderful,
3	unsearchable, beyond my reach ...

4	the breadth,
4,3	and length,
4,3,2	and height,
4,3,2,1	and depth!

1	Who will separate us from the love of Christ?
2	Will hardship or distress,
3	or persecution, or famine,
4	or nakedness or peril or sword?

2	No, in all these things we are more than conquerors through the One who loved us.
1	I am convinced that neither death, nor life, nor angels, nor rulers, nor things present, nor things to come, nor powers, nor height, nor depth, nor anything else in all creation will be able to separate us from the love of God in Christ Jesus our Lord ...

4	the breadth,
3	and length,
2	and height,
1	and depth!

1	O the depth of the riches
1,2	and wisdom
1,2,3	and knowledge
1,2,3,4	and love of God!

Adapted from Ephesians 3:14-19; Psalm 139:1-12; and Romans 8:35-39; 11:33.

42. Awake, Rise, and Christ will Shine on You

Background

I created this reading for the opening session of an evangelism conference whose theme was drawn from Ephesians 5:14-15: "Awake, rise, and Christ will shine on you! Live wisely, making the most of the time!" To develop this theme, I included portions of Isaiah 58, Matthew 5, and 2 Corinthians 4, which use the image of light to speak of God's work among us and our task in the world. Also included are the first lines of a folk hymn we used as an opening song, "Here in This Place."

Rehearsal Notes

Encourage the four readers to speak with enthusiasm and zeal. They are delivering a wake-up call!

At the places where speakers read together, the intention is to add volume and emphasis. Rehearse these lines until readers are comfortable with the rhythm and flow.

Near the end of the reading, there is a sentence where voices are "added" as the first reader continues to speak. In this case, the first reader is the leader and should read the whole sentence in a normal rhythm. The other readers should join, matching the first person's rhythm and tone, though increasing the overall volume.

Worship Planning

This reading will work best as a call to worship, followed by the song cited in the script, "Here in This Place." If that hymn is unfamiliar, you might use "Sleepers, Wake!" or "Awake, Awake, Fling Off the Night."

Awake, Rise, and Christ Will Shine on You

1	Awake, sleeper!
2	Rise from the dead!
3	And Christ will shine on you!
4	Live wisely, making the most of the time!
1	Awake!
2	Rise!
3	And Christ will shine on you!
4	Your light shall break forth like the morning!
3	God's healing will spring up in a moment!
2	Righteousness will go before you!
1	God's glory will follow behind!
3	You will call to your God
2	and the Lord will answer.
3	You will cry and God will say,
1,2,4	"Here I am!"
3	Here!
1	in *this* place,
2	new light is streaming;
4	now is the darkness vanished away.
3	See!
1	in *this* space,
2	our fears and our dreamings
4	are brought here to God in the light of this day.
3	Gather us in—the lost and forsaken,
1	gather us in—the blind and the lame,
2	gather us in—and we shall awaken,
4	we shall arise at the sound of our name!
1,2	Awake!
3,4	Rise!
1	And Christ will shine on you!
3	Live wisely, making the most of the time!

4	For once you were darkness, but now you are light in the Lord.
3	Walk as children of light— bearing fruit that is good and right and true.

1	You are the light of the world!
2	A city on a hill can't be hid.
1	No one puts a cover over a lamp, but rather stands it up, to give light to the whole room!
2	Let your light shine so that people see your good works and give glory to God!
1,2	Awake!
3,4	Rise!
1	And Christ will shine on you!
3	Live wisely, making the most of the time!

1	For what we preach is not ourselves, but Jesus Christ as Lord,
2	with ourselves as your servants for Jesus' sake.
3	For it is the God who said, "Let light shine out of darkness"
4	who has shone in our hearts
3, 4	to give the light of the knowledge
2,3,4	of the glory of God
1,2,3,4	in the face of Christ.

4	Here in this place new light is streaming.
1	Awake, sleeper!
2	Rise from the dead!
3	And Christ will shine on you!
4	Live wisely, making the most of the time!
1	Awake!
2	Rise!
3	And Christ will shine on you!

Adapted from Ephesians 5:8-9, 14-15; Isaiah 58:8-9; Matthew 5:14-16; 2 Corinthians 4:5-6; and stanza 1 of "Here in This Place" ("Gather Us In," Copyright © 1982 by GIA Publications Inc.).

Other Resources

43. God Is Our Song
44. An Undaunted Divine Comedy
45. Benediction

43. God Is Our Song

Background

From Miriam at the Red Sea (Exodus 15) to King David (2 Samuel 6) to Jesus after the Last Supper (Mark 14) to the saints at the end of history (Revelation 14), we hear the ongoing song of God's people, singing the Lord's praise. This reading invites us to join that great chorus in testifying that "God is our strength and song" (Isaiah 12:2).

Rehearsal Notes

This script presents four biblical texts which highlight the use of song as a response of praise and prayer. Each text should be read in a way that seeks to paint a picture of that scene for the audience.

    The two-line refrain should be repeated with enthusiasm and joy as the continuing thread that ties the scenes together. The last time this line is spoken, three voices read together; rehearse this line until the readers can speak with confidence and ease.

Worship Planning

This reading could be easily used as an opening call to worship before a hymn of praise such as "Sing Praise to God Who Reigns," which picks up the theme of singing.

    It could also be used in a service that explores how certain hymns carry our theology and our memories of significant moments in our spiritual journey. Invite three or four persons to share brief reflections on a favorite hymn and its importance for their faith understanding and experience. Then sing that hymn after each reflection. No need for a sermon—the Word will be proclaimed in reflection and song!

    As a call to worship, use a psalm that focuses on singing (for example, Psalm 92:1-4 or Psalm 96:1-6). Choose an opening and closing hymn based on music as a theme: "When in Our Music God Is Glorified" or "My Life Flows On." Colossians 3:16-17 would make a good benediction.

God Is Our Song

1   God is my strength and my song!

2   The Lord has become my salvation!

1   Then Miriam, the prophetess, the sister of Moses,
took a timbrel in her hand;
and all the women went out after her with timbrels and dancing.
And Miriam sang to them:
Sing to the Lord, for God has triumphed gloriously;
the horse and rider God has thrown into the sea.

3   God is our strength and our song!

4   The Lord has become our salvation!

2   So King David went and brought up the ark of God from the house
of Obed-edom to the city of David with rejoicing ...
and David danced before the Lord with all his might!
... So David and all the house of Israel
brought up the ark of the Lord
with shouts of joy and the sound of the trumpet.

4   God is my strength and my song!

1   The Lord has become my salvation!

3   And as they were eating, Jesus took bread
and blessed and broke it and gave it to them and said,
"Take, this is my body."
And he took a cup, and when he had given thanks,
he gave it to them ... and said,
"This is my blood of the covenant, which is poured out for many...."
And when they had sung a hymn, they went out to the Mount of Olives.

2   God is our strength and our song.

1   The Lord has become our salvation.

4   Then I looked, and lo, on Mount Zion stood the Lamb,
and with him a hundred and forty-four thousand....
And I heard a voice from heaven like the sound of many waters
and like the sound of loud thunder;
the voice I heard was like the sound of harpers playing on their harps,
and they sing a new song before the throne
and before the four living creatures and before the elders.

1,2,3	God is our strength and our song.
4	The Lord has become our salvation.

Adapted from Isaiah 12:2; Exodus 15:20-21; 2 Samuel 6:12-15; Mark 14:22-26; and Revelation 14:1-3.

44. An Undaunted Divine Comedy

Background

This presentation develops the theme of laughter and comedy as a clue to God's ways with the world. It explores "the folly of what we preach ... the foolishness of God" (1 Corinthians 1:21-25). Theologians have often explored the connection between humor and human understandings of God. See most recently Conrad Hyers' *And God Created Laughter: The Bible as Divine Comedy* (Atlanta, Ga.: John Knox Press, 1987).

This script takes some lighthearted liberty in interpreting certain texts, but its intention is to present a joyful, truthful rendition of the gospel message. May it remind us that the world belongs to God and that, as God's children, we live with delight within the circle of God's sovereignty and redemption.

Rehearsal Notes

This script is structured for four readers, but can also be read as a monologue. The reading should be presented in dramatic narrative style; it tells the biblical story from Genesis to Revelation.

There are numerous puns and jokes in the script. Rehearse often enough so that readers can "play" with the lines, giving expression and emphasis to these humorous elements. Identify the lines that are likely to elicit laughter and remind readers to allow the audience time to laugh! Then, enjoy yourselves!

Worship Planning

I first used this reading in a service on April Fools Day, using 1 Corinthians 1:18-25 as a text and singing "Joy to the World" and "Lord of the Dance" (*Sing and Rejoice!* No. 67). Other biblical texts that mention laughter could be used as part of a call to worship or benediction (Psalm 126; Ecclesiastes 3:2-4; Luke 6:21; Genesis 21:1-7). This reading could be used during Lent, or perhaps more suitably on the first Sunday after Easter as a way of expressing resurrection joy and confidence.

An Undaunted Divine Comedy

1   In the beginning, when God created the heavens and the earth,
the earth was without form and void, darkness and chaos.

2   And God laughed, "Let there be light!"
And there was light and it was good!

3   And God laughed, "Let there be firmament, land and trees,
sun, moon, and stars, animals and birds!"
And they appeared. And it was good.

4   And God laughed, "Let us create humankind in our image!"
Male and female, God created them.

2   And when the man and woman saw each other,
they laughed, "Bone of my bone, flesh of my flesh!
What a delight! Let's go play!"

3   And God said,
"Be fruitful, multiply, fill the earth and subdue it!
But remember to laugh—
for the earth does belong to me, and you are my creatures."

4   And the snake said, "Get serious! Get down to business!
How would you calculate your return if you ate this fruit?"

1   And the man and woman got serious,
and they ate from the tree of solemnity and sobriety.
And God said, "This is not funny!
In fact, this is a *grave* matter!"
And life became difficult and serious.

2   And God said to a very old man and woman,
"You shall have a son!"

3   And they said, "You've got to be *kidding*!"

2   And God said, "Yes, I am.
So you shall call him Isaac—that is laughter!"

4   And so the God of Abraham, Laughter, and Jacob continued
to lead people into the comedy of their lives.

2   And God said to Moses, "Go tell Pharaoh to let my people go
so they can play in the wilderness!"

1   And Moses said, "All that trouble just to pray?"

2   And God said, "No—play, not pray!
Let them come before me with singing, with shouts of joy;
let them dance before the Lord. Let them play!"

3   And Pharaoh said, "This is serious business!
You have work to do! Besides, we are in charge!
No work, no play!"

4   But God brought them across the Red Sea
with a ripple of laughter.
God liberated them with laughter
and they entered the Promised Land of justice, jokes, and joy!

1   And the prophets said, "You've gotten too serious!
Don't you remember—the earth is the Lord's!
Laugh a little—and share!"

2   And the prophets said,
"You are taking yourselves far too seriously!
Don't build yourselves strongholds—trust in the Lord!"

3   And the prophets said, "You are far too serious!
Remember that you are all God's creatures—
rich and poor, northerner, southerner.
Treat each other with justice!
Worship the Lord—and have a party!"

4   And the people said, "If we aren't serious
about ourselves, our security, our society,
we won't survive...!"

3   And they were carried away into exile.

1   In the beginning was the Word.
And the Word was a word of joy and laughter!
The Word was with God; and the Word was God.
When God created the world, that Word of wisdom was dancing:

2   it "danced in the morning when the world was begun!
[it] danced in the moon and the stars and the sun;
[it] came down from heaven and [it] danced on the earth."[8]

3   And that Word of joy and laughter
became flesh and dwelt among us full of grace and truth.

4   The light shines in the darkness and says, "Lighten up!"

1   They looked for a god—and they found a baby!

2   They looked for a king—and found a servant!

3   They looked for someone who would have
dominion, and power and glory!

4   And they found a poor, traveling prophet
who healed the sick, cared for the needy,
and let the children come unto him.

1   But he laughed with authority and with great abandon!

2   They ran out of wine—and he said,
"Fill the jars to overflowing!"

3	They ran out of bread—and he fed the five thousand.
4	They wanted to throw him a proper banquet, and he ate with publicans and prostitutes and sinners.
3	And they said, "You aren't serious about the kingdom! You can't really mean for us to laugh and live this way! It's foolishness!"

1	So they crucified him—and laughter died.
2	And God said, "The joke is on you!"
3	And Satan said, "You should have seen the one that *god* away!"
4	And laughter was resurrected from the grave!

2	And Mary was sitting in the garden weeping, and she did not recognize Jesus standing before her!
4	And Jesus laughed!
2	And she said, "My teacher! I have seen the Lord!"

1	And the Spirit of laughter came upon them like a mighty wind, like giggling tongues of fire!
2	And the faith spread like a funny joke from coast to coast,
3	"Did you hear the one about Jesus— who laughed in the face of death! And was victorious!"
4	And many laughed! And many believed!

1	And the Spirit of joy and laughter said, "Lo! I am with you always!
2	Until the creation of a new heaven and a new earth!...
3	when God's dwelling will be with all the people!
4	when the only tears will be tears of laughter
1	and the only mourning will be joy in the morning!...
2	when crying and death and pain will be no more!
3	But all will be celebration and riddles of delight."
4	In the beginning and at the end—laughter!

⁸From "Lord of the Dance," by Sydney Carter, © 1963 by Galliard Ltd.(*Sing and Rejoice!* No. 67).

Written on 25 January 1989. Dedicated with deep affection to one of my professors in graduate school, Kent Harold Richards, who first helped me see what a playground of adventure and delight biblical exegesis could be. There are allusions in this poem to the work of other biblical scholars and artists. Two I will cite as most obvious to me: Sydney Carter's lyric "Lord of the Dance" and Conrad Hyers' book And God Created Laughter.

45. Benediction

Background

This benediction combines words of sending with hand motions, thus emphasizing the call to embody the gospel message. The threefold benediction (Stand ... go ... commit ...) with motions is repeated three times, the last time in silent prayer, as those participating are invited to let the words sink deeply into their minds and hearts.

Rehearsal Notes

The leader should rehearse the benediction several times, so that it can be introduced and explained to the congregation with ease. Optimally, the whole benediction could be memorized. But if you use notes, be sure to make arrangements to have your hands totally free; it is important that you are able to model all the hand motions. If presented smoothly, the final silent enactment of this benediction will be a powerful expression of corporate prayer.

Worship Planning

This benediction can be adapted to different themes by modifying the content, while keeping the basic structure and motions. For example, an alternative wording that could be used with the same motions:

> Stand in solidarity with each other as brothers and sisters,
>   fully alive before God.
> Go in determination to witness boldly, to grow into a person
>   who reflects God's glory.
> Commit yourselves to reach out with the compassion of Christ,
>   to embrace the world with God's love.

Benediction

Leader: *{Invite the congregation to stand.}*
Our benediction is one we will act out, not only here with hand
motions but also as we leave this place to live in faithful service.

We will repeat three motions three times—twice, as I
say the words of benediction, and the third time, in silence.

*{THE FIRST TIME, give instructions about the motions as you say the words of bene-
diction and demonstrate each motion.}*
First, hold hands with the persons beside you,
as a sign that we STAND IN SOLIDARITY WITH EACH OTHER,
UNITED IN CHRIST, THE PRINCE OF PEACE.

{Pause}
Then, raise your hands to shoulder height,
in the shape of fists, but palms forward,
as a sign of our DETERMINATION TO WITNESS BOLDLY,
TO ACT WITH COURAGE AND TO TAKE RISKS
AS WE WORK FOR PEACE AND JUSTICE.

{pause}
Finally, extend your arms with open hands, reaching out to the sky, as a
sign of your COMMITMENT TO REACH OUT WITH THE COMPASSION
OF CHRIST, TO EMBRACE THE WORLD WITH GOD'S LOVE.

{THE SECOND TIME, say the words of benediction as you do the motions.}
Let us enact this benediction as I say it for a second time.

{Holding hands}
STAND IN SOLIDARITY WITH EACH OTHER,
UNITED IN CHRIST, THE PRINCE OF PEACE.

{Fists raised to shoulders}
GO IN DETERMINATION TO WITNESS BOLDLY, TO ACT WITH
COURAGE, TO TAKE RISKS AS YOU WORK FOR PEACE AND JUSTICE.

{Arms extended upward}
COMMIT YOURSELVES TO REACH OUT WITH THE COMPASSION
OF CHRIST, TO EMBRACE THE WORLD WITH GOD'S LOVE.

{THE THIRD TIME, do the benediction in silence.}
And once more in silence.

*{Lead the sequence of three motions, with a brief silence between each motion to
allow time for silent prayer.}*
Amen.

III

Songs

Part III: Songs

1. Love the Lord (With All)
2. Philippian Hymn
3. Prayer for Peace
4. Love Suffers Much
5. Joy Wasn't in Me
6. Enlarge Your Tent
7. Micah
8. Jerusalem
9. The Light Shines in the Darkness
10. Arise, Shine
11. John Nine
12. Many Gifts
13. Love Song
14. God's People
15. Communion Song
16. Benediction

1. Love the Lord (With All)

Patricia J. Shelly

Patricia J. Shelly
arr. by Marilyn Houser Hamm

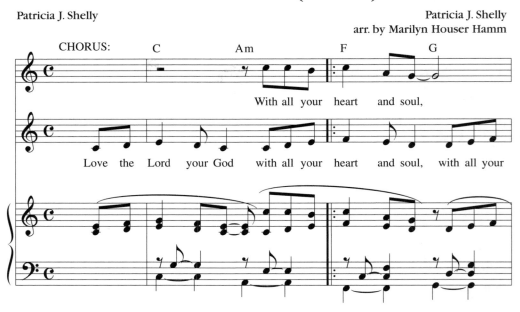

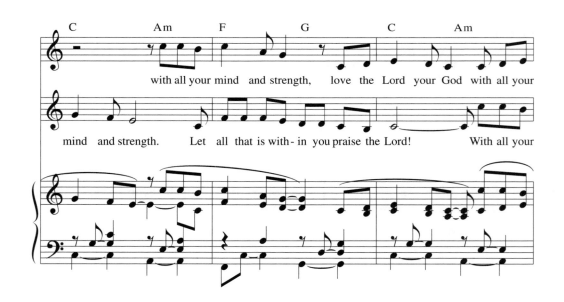

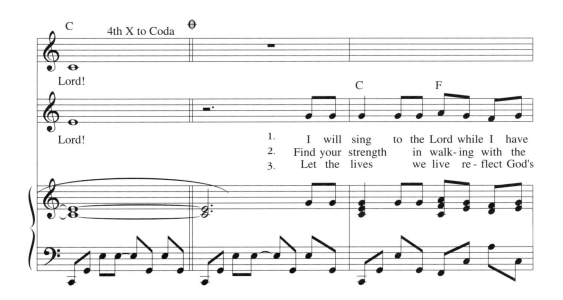

1. Love the Lord (With All)

The Great Commandment enjoins us to love God with our whole being. In our temptation to separate God from our living and our learning, and to compartmentalize our faith, we may find it difficult to let this truth permeate our lives. Yet this commandment resonates from Deuteronomy to the Psalter, from the Gospels to the letters of Paul: love God with heart, soul, mind, and strength. (Deuteronomy 6:4-5; Psalm 103:1; Mark 12:28-34; Ephesians 3:16-19)

2. Philippian Hymn

Patricia J. Shelly

Patricia J. Shelly
arr. by J. Harold Moyer

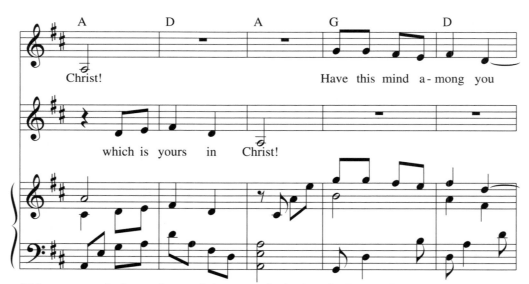

This song works best when soloists or a choir sing the "verses."

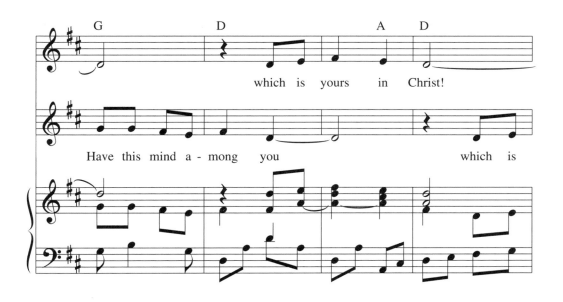

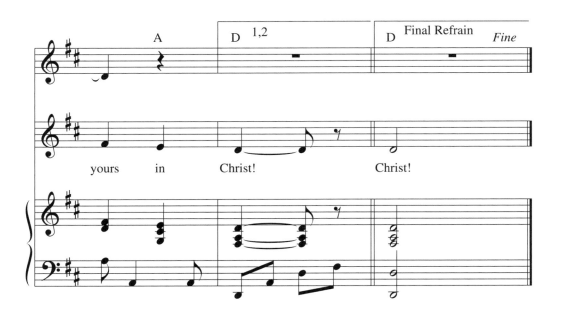

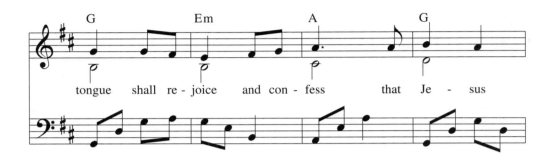

tongue shall re - joice and con - fess that Je - sus

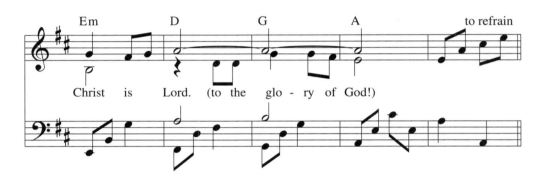

Christ is Lord. (to the glo - ry of God!)

2. Philippian Hymn

Most scholars believe that in Philippians 2:5-11 Paul quoted an ancient hymn text as encouragement to his readers to share the attitude of Christ. This was not the last time that a preacher found the words of a hymn worth citing in a sermon or teaching! This song allows us to sing the ancient hymn once again, and to reflect on what it means to "have the mind of Christ."

In a congregational setting, divide the congregation into two sections to sing the chorus, and have soloists or a choir (women—stanza 1, men—stanza 2) sing the verses. Print the refrain in a bulletin to facilitate congregational participation in the song.

Congregational Refrain for "Philippian Hymn"

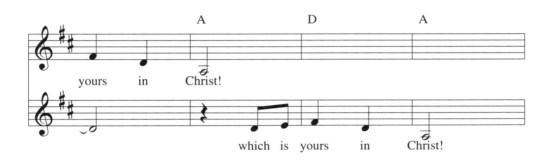

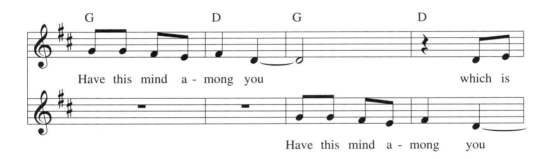

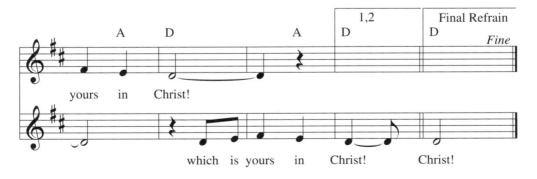

3. Prayer for Peace

Patricia J. Shelly

Patricia J. Shelly
arr. by J. Harold Moyer

Strength-en the hands of those who work for peace,

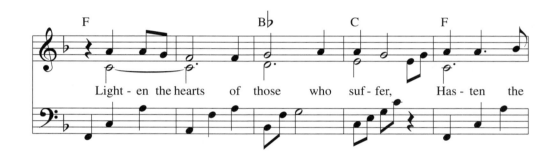

Light - en the hearts of those who suf - fer, Has - ten the

day that sees your jus - tice done, God, may your king - dom

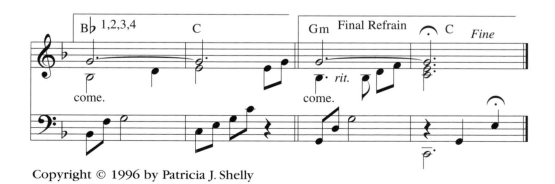

come.   come.

1. God of heav - en and earth,
2. Je - sus, full - ness of God,
3. Spir - it, pres - ence and power,
4. Yours the earth, and heaven,

God of jus - tice and truth.
Lib - er - a - tor and Lord!
Spir - it of strug - gle and hope!
Yours the king - dom and power,

Friend of the poor, Source of all love,
Suf - fer - ing ser - vant, Prince of peace,
Coun - sel - or, Com - for - ter,
Yours the glo - ry ev - er - more,

to refrain

hear us as we pray:
lead us in your way:
teach us how to pray:
God of here and now:

3. Prayer for Peace

This song is a prayer for peace and justice. Every year this call seems more urgent. The verses address the Trinity (Creator, Christ, Spirit) in ways that affirm that the creator and advocate of peace is the God revealed to us in Jesus Christ. The petitions affirm the connection between worship and peacemaking. This song is deeply rooted in my experience at an ecumenical, international gathering in Seoul, Korea. After humming the chorus for several years, I finally finished the song while planning a worship service for the 1990 Mennonite World Conference in Winnipeg, Manitoba. (Matthew 5:9; 6:9-13; Psalm 146; Luke 4:18-21; John 14:26-27)

4. Love Suffers Much

This song was born out of personal experience as well as the difficult news that some dear friends had been diagnosed with diseases that were sure to prove fatal. I needed to know again that God could embrace such pain, that the faith community could hear such pain and not turn away. I needed to affirm again that such experiences can, by the grace of God, deepen our awareness of the suffering all around us and enable us to show compassion and be comforted. (Ecclesiastes 3:4; 1 Corinthians 13:7; Matthew 5:4; Psalm 103:8)

4. Love Suffers Much

Patricia J. Shelly   Patricia J. Shelly

CHORUS:
Come feel the pain in your life: it can o-pen your heart to the

suff-'ring of the whole wide world. Come feel the pain in your life: it can

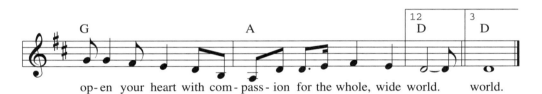

op-en your heart with com-pass-ion for the whole, wide world. world.

1. There is a time for weep-ing and a time for tears; there is a
2. It is love that suf-fers much and still be-lieves, when you
3. Oh the Lord is merc-i-ful, the Lord is good, and our

kind of heal-ing that be-gins when we share each oth-er's
show com-pass-ion then you shall re-ceive the bless-ed
God is weep-ing for the pain of the world, for God is

bur - dens and hopes and fears.
com - fort of those who grieve.
love, and pain is un-der-stood.

Copyright © 1996 by Patricia J. Shelly

5. Joy Wasn't in Me

Much as Psalm 137 is a song about a people in exile who could not sing, this poem sings the Lord's song in the foreign land of cold winters and darkness. The song of faith perseveres in the midst of trial and difficulty! Although there are no explicit biblical references here, the song captures the rhythm of lament and hope in a psalm like Psalm 42. Even "at night, God's song is with me, a prayer to the God of my life." (Psalm 42)

5. Joy Wasn't in Me

Patricia J. Shelly   Patricia J. Shelly

1. Joy was - n't in me to - day, no it was - n't, no Joy was - n't in me to - day.
2. I will live through the win - ter and sing my sad - ness, I will live through the win - ter and sing.
3. And my song chang - es dark - ness to light, hear the mu - sic, and my song chang - es dark - ness to light.

I have but - toned my coat, there's a cold wind a - blow-ing, when it ev - er will end I have no way of know - ing and
I know soon comes the time for the change of the sea - sons, I have hope for the warmth it will bring. I will
For Joy brings the sun - rise so brill - iant - ly shin - ing that I think I am glad for the night. And my

Joy was - n't in me to - day, no it was - n't, no Joy was - n't in me to - day.
live through the win - ter and sing my sad - ness, I will live through the win - ter and sing.
song chang - es dark - ness to light, hear the mu - sic, and my song chang - es dark - ness to light.

6. Enlarge Your Tent

Isaiah 54
Patricia J. Shelly

Patricia J. Shelly

6. Enlarge Your Tent

This song was commissioned for the 1985 joint sessions of the Western District (General Conference Mennonite) and Rocky Mountain (Mennonite Church) conferences in Boulder, Colorado. The song's initial imagery comes from Isaiah 54, but in many ways it is an affirmation of the Great Commission—God's call for us to participate in the spreading of the gospel, the enlarging of the tent of faith, the extension of boundaries beyond our feeble imaginations. (Isaiah 54:1-3; Matthew 5:13-16; 6:33; Luke 4:18-21)

7. Micah

Patricia J. Shelly

Patricia J. Shelly

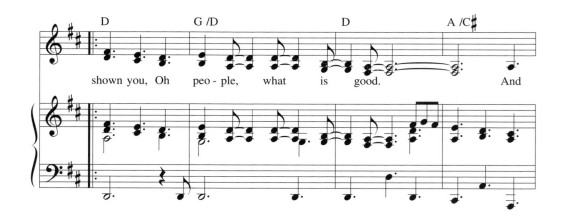

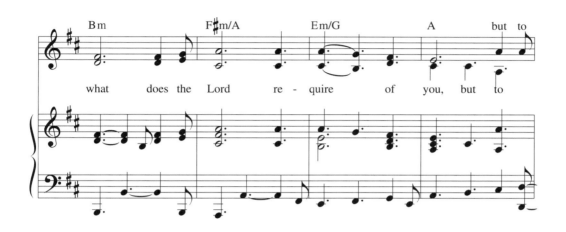

what does the Lord re - quire of you, but to

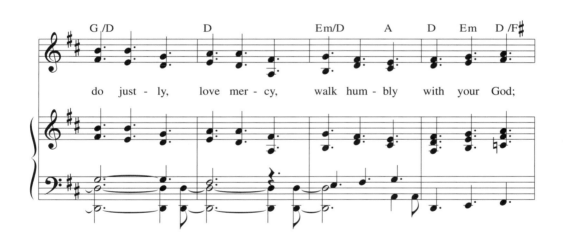

do just - ly, love mer - cy, walk hum - bly with your God;

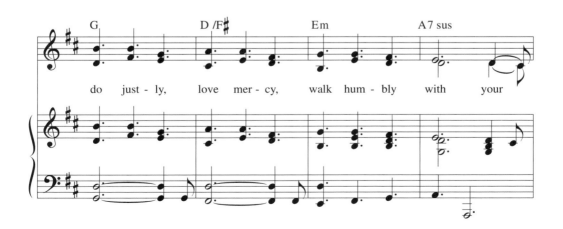

do just - ly, love mer - cy, walk hum - bly with your

Lord is a God for - giv - ing and faith - ful,
jus - tice come flow - ing like ten thou - sand riv - ers.

stead - fast with thou - sands in in - fin - ite
When you show mer - cy, in mer - cy you'll

love. God has
live. God has

7. Micah

The prophet Amos called his community to seek the Lord. Micah asks, "What does the Lord seek (require) of you?" In both instances the Hebrew word for seek (require) is the same. For both prophets the message is the same: the true worship of God is in doing justice, embracing mercy, and seeking the Lord. (Micah 6:8; Amos 5:4-6, 24; Exodus 34:6-7; Matthew 5:7)

8. Jerusalem

Besides being a beloved city, the biblical Jerusalem is a symbol for God's presence, a place where somehow God is more real. Many hopes and dreams are attached to this city. But what happens to us when our dreams and visions and our most cherished hopes are challenged, violated, or destroyed? Can we respond without resorting to violence as a means of protection or revenge? How can we remember the past—even the experience of suffering and pain—in a way that does not paralyze the present or destroy the future? (Psalm 137; Micah 3:9-11; Luke 13:34; 19:41; Revelation 21:2-4; Hebrews 11:10)

8. Jerusalem

Psalm 137
Patricia J. Shelly

Patricia J. Shelly

9. The Light Shines in the Darkness

The story of the incarnation in John's Gospel does not include shepherds, wise men, stables, and stars. It does include the brilliant affirmation that God's light shines in the darkness and is not overcome by it. This is a song to be sung whenever the times are bad and our lives are full of darkness. (John 1:5, 9)

9. The Light Shines in the Darkness

John 1:5
Patricia J. Shelly

Patricia J. Shelly
arr. by Marilyn Houser Hamm

*Chords for guitar accompaniment alone

2. Those watching sheep in the cold grass all alone
Have seen the sign and it fills their hearts with hope.

3. Three traveling souls searching near and looking far
Say the light still shines: for they've seen a brilliant star.

4. The times are bad and we walk into the night,
But the darkness we feel only helps us see the light.

5. The true light that shines in every person's life
Is coming into the world. Come and celebrate the sight!

10. Arise, Shine

This is a Christmas song, but we should sing of "God-with-us" throughout the year! The message of the third verse is that God's presence spans geographical distance, historical distance, and designated holidays! (Isaiah 60:1, 19; Revelation 21:22; 22:5)

10. Arise, Shine

Patricia J. Shelly

Patricia J. Shelly
arr. by Dennis Friesen-Carper

Em   A   F#m   Bm   C#dim

1. A dark - ened world so full of gloom; an inn so
2. A peo - ple wait - ing for a sign that hope is ful -
3. Come and see what the an - gels tell; that God is
4. The sun will no long-er shine by day, the moon will not

F#7   Bm   D/A   Em   A   F#m

crowd - ed there is - n't room; but God will come in hu - man
filled a prom - ised time. A man and wom-an who jour - ney
with us Em - man - u - el. Long a - go in Beth - le -
glow when ev - 'ning comes, but God will be your last - ing

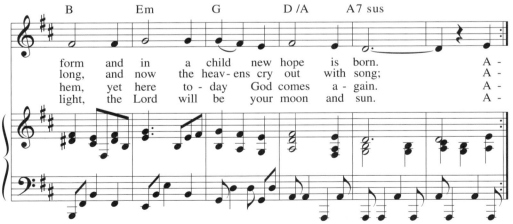

B   Em   G   D/A   A7 sus

form and in a child new hope is born. A -
long, and now the heav-ens cry out with song; A -
hem, yet here to - day God comes a - gain. A -
light, the Lord will be your moon and sun. A -

11. John Nine

Patricia J. Shelly

Patricia J. Shelly
arr. by Dennis Friesen-Carper

1. As he went on his way, Je-sus saw a blind beg-gar, and
2. The blind man was healed and the Phar-i-sees doubt-ed that
3. The Phar-i-sees cried, "Are you say-ing we're blind?" And

blind-ness was sin in that so-ci-e-ty. Je-sus
this was of God that a blind man could teach. They
Je-sus said, "If you were blind you'd go free. But

said, "Go wash, and new sight you'll be gi-ven.
called for the neigh-bors, they called for the par-ents, the
now that you claim to have sight you are guil-ty, your

I am the Light of the world," said He.
beg-gar said, "Once I was blind, now I see!"
vis-ion is blind-ness, how dark it must be!"

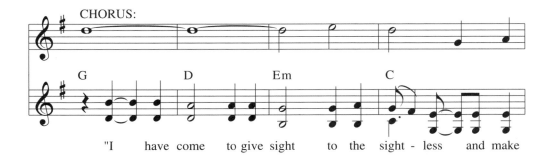

CHORUS:

G D Em C

"I have come to give sight to the sight - less and make

D Em

blind those who think they can see.

G D Em C

I have come to give sight to the sight - less and make

D E

blind those who think they can see."

11. John Nine

Jesus told a parable that fits with this story very well: "The eye is the lamp of the body. So if your eye is sound, your whole body will be full of light. But if your eye is not sound, your whole body will be full of darkness. If then the light in you is darkness, how great is the darkness!" (John 9; Matthew 6:22-23)

12. Many Gifts

As a Mennonite, I wrote this song for a Methodist church service celebrating the ministry of laypeople in the church! This song itself was a fusion of many gifts. Such diversity can sometimes be a painful challenge for the church—as Paul found out with the church at Corinth. But it is surely cause for celebration as well. Many tasks, many talents, many gifts—but the church looks for unity in the Spirit. (1 Corinthians 12)

12. Many Gifts

Patricia J. Shelly

Patricia J. Shelly
arr. by Dennis Friesen-Carper

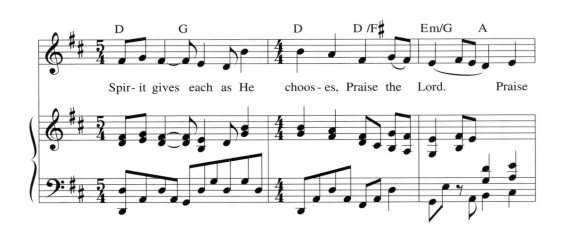

13. Love Song

1 Corinthians 13
Patricia J. Shelly

Patricia J. Shelly

13. Love Song

What is it that binds together the diversity of gifts in the church
(see 1 Corinthians 12)? What is "the more excellent way"? Perhaps
we should sing this as a riddle: What is patient and kind? What is
slow to anger? What believes all things, hopes all things, bears all
things? This way we would let Paul's definition shape our understanding of love, rather than seeing love as a romantic ideal.

(1 Corinthians 13)

14. God's People

Patricia J. Shelly

Patricia J. Shelly

Once you were no peo - ple, Now you are God's Peo - ple,

sing prais - es to the Lord! Once you had no mer - cy,

Now you've re-ceived mer - cy. Sing prais - es to the Lord!

1. You are a cho - sen race, a roy - al priest - hood,
2. Show your - selves God's Peo - ple, live as God's chil - dren,

a ho - ly nat - ion, the peo - ple of God.
shin - ing like lights in the midst of the world.

To sing the prais - es of One who had called you
Stand fast in one spir - it, hold forth the word of life,

out of the dark - ness and in - to the Light!
walk side by side and re - joice in the Lord!

14. God's People

The prophet Hosea spoke about separation from God by naming his child "Not-my-People." Then Hosea spoke about God's redemption in a promise to rename the child "You are my people." The writer of 1 Peter adopted this imagery, as well as that of Exodus 19, to talk about our redemption in Christ. In both testaments, being God's people is not a prize or award—it is a calling to be a "light to the nations," to witness and to serve. (Hosea 1:8-9; 2:23; Exodus 19:5-6; 1 Peter 2:9-10; Philippians 1:27; 2:15-16)

15. Communion Song

Patricia J. Shelly

Patricia J. Shelly
arr. by Dennis Friesen Carper

1. Do this and know that you are my peo - ple. Do this and know that you are loved,
2. Do this and know that I am a-mong you, And I'll be with you when you call.

Do this and re-mem-ber that you love one an-oth - er, And be at peace, and be at peace.
Do this and re-mem-ber that I've called you my peo - ple, To serve the world, to serve the world.

The ta - ble of the Lord is set be - fore you with bread and wine to feed your soul.
This is the bread my bod - y bro - ken, I give to you, re - mem - ber me.

Now hear the word Christ speaks a - mong you; God's pres - ence here will make you whole.
This is the cup, my life o'er-flow-ing in - to the world, Re - mem - ber me.

*Guitar chords for unison singing only

15. Communion Song

This communion song emphasizes the celebration of the Lord's Supper as the gathering of the members of the body of Christ. Jesus asked that when we eat the bread and drink the cup, we remember him and remember our calling as God's people to serve the world. (1 Corinthians 11:23-25; 10:16-17)

16. Benediction

This benediction speaks of both the challenges we face in our ongoing life journey as well as the never-ending love and grace of God in which we abide. It echoes in structure and theme the benediction of Aaron in Numbers 6. I have recently realized that there is also a faint echo of the Tommy Dorsey hymn "Precious Lord, take my hand, lead me on, let me stand…." (Numbers 6:24-26)

16. Benediction

Patricia J. Shelly

Patricia J. Shelly
arr. by Dennis Friesen-Carper

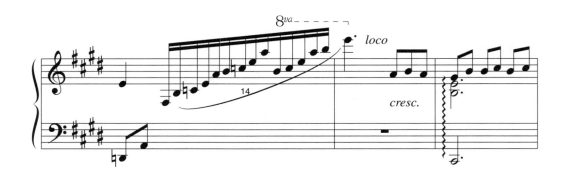

The Lord lift you up, the Lord take your hand, the Lord lead you forth, and cause you to stand, se-cure in God's Word, seek-ing God's face, a-bound-ing in love, a-bid-ing in grace.

Scripture Index

Text	**Readers Theater Script**
Genesis 1:1-2	33. The Spirit of God (Reading 1)
Genesis 28:10-19	12. Lord, You Have Searched Me
Exodus 15:20-21	43. God Is Our Song
Deuteronomy 6:1-12	4. With All Your Strength
Deuteronomy 6:4-7, 10-12	1. With Thankful Hearts
Deuteronomy 6:10-12	8. Know and Serve the Lord with Gladness
Deuteronomy 8:17-18	1. With Thankful Hearts
Deuteronomy 8:17-18	4. With All Your Strength
Deuteronomy 8:17-18	8. Know and Serve the Lord with Gladness
Deuteronomy 10:12, 17-19	4. With All Your Strength
Joshua 4:1-7	17. What Do These Stones Mean?
2 Samuel 6:12-15	43. God Is Our Song
1 Chronicles 28:9	8. Know and Serve the Lord with Gladness
Psalm 6:6-7	15. Through the Valley of the Shadow
Psalm 13:1-3	15. Through the Valley of the Shadow
Psalm 19:1	6. A Modern Psalm: Call to Praise
Psalm 23	13. Two Worlds of Experience
Psalm 23	16. Responsive Reading on Psalm 23 and the Beatitudes
Psalm 23:4	15. Through the Valley of the Shadow
Psalm 42	13. Two Worlds of Experience
Psalm 46:1	19. Seek the Lord: Micah and the Prophets
Psalm 46:1-3, 7	29. Ask, Seek, Knock
Psalm 46:1-3, 10-11	10. God Is Our Refuge and Strength
Psalm 62	14. A Cry from the Depths
Psalm 90:1, 17	17. What Do These Stones Mean?
Psalm 90:1-2, 14	11. How Can We Sing in a Strange New Land?
Psalm 90:12	21. A Heart of Wisdom
Psalm 96:1, 11-12	6. A Modern Psalm: Call to Praise
Psalm 100	8. Know and Serve the Lord with Gladness
Psalm 100:1-2	19. Seek the Lord: Micah and the Prophets
Psalm 100:3-5	1. With Thankful Hearts
Psalm 100:4	30. A Thanksgiving Reading
Psalm 103:1-5	30. A Thanksgiving Reading
Psalm 103:1-5	7. Bless the Lord, O My Soul
Psalm 104:24, 30	33. The Spirit of God (Reading 1)
Psalm 105:4	19. Seek the Lord: Micah and the Prophets

Psalm 111:1	1. With Thankful Hearts
Psalm 130	14. A Cry from the Depths
Psalm 130	26. The People Who Walk in Darkness
Psalm 137:1-4	11. How Can We Sing in a Strange New Land?
Psalm 139:1-12	41. The Breadth and Length and Height and Depth
Psalm 139:1-12, 23-24	12. Lord, You Have Searched Me
Psalm 143:5, 8	22. What Is New, What Is Old
Psalm 145:3	21. A Heart of Wisdom
Psalm 145:3-5, 10-12	9. Declare God's Marvelous Works
Psalm 146:5-9	10. God Is Our Refuge and Strength
Psalm 148:3, 9-12	6. A Modern Psalm: Call to Praise
Psalm 150:6	6. A Modern Psalm: Call to Praise
Proverbs 1:20-21	3. Treasuring God's Wisdom
Proverbs 2:1-11	3. Treasuring God's Wisdom
Proverbs 3:13-14, 19-20	21. A Heart of Wisdom
Isaiah 9:2, 6-7	26. The People Who Walk in Darkness
Isaiah 12:2	43. God Is Our Song
Isaiah 30:15-18	19. Seek the Lord: Micah and the Prophets
Isaiah 40:3-5	20. Behold! I Make All Things New!
Isaiah 41:10	15. Through the Valley of the Shadow
Isaiah 43:1-2	15. Through the Valley of the Shadow
Isaiah 43:10	38. Christ Is Our Peace (Reading 1)
Isaiah 43:15-21	20. Behold! I Make All Things New!
Isaiah 43:18	22. What Is New, What Is Old
Isaiah 46:8-10	22. What Is New, What Is Old
Isaiah 55:6-7	19. Seek the Lord: Micah and the Prophets
Isaiah 58:8-9	42. Awake, Rise, and Christ will Shine on You
Isaiah 58:8-10	11. How Can We Sing in a Strange New Land?
Isaiah 65:17-18	22. What Is New, What Is Old
Jeremiah 17:7-8	23. Parable of the Sower
Hosea 11:1-4, 7, 8-9	19. Seek the Lord: Micah and the Prophets
Joel 2:28-29	33. The Spirit of God (Reading 1)
Amos 2:6-7	19. Seek the Lord: Micah and the Prophets
Amos 5:4, 14-15, 24	19. Seek the Lord: Micah and the Prophets
Micah 6	18. Micah 6: A Dramatic Paraphrase
Micah 6:8	19. Seek the Lord: Micah and the Prophets
Wisdom of Solomon 6:17-20	21. A Heart of Wisdom
Wisdom of Solomon 7:22-28	21. A Heart of Wisdom

Matthew 1:18-20	27. Ancient Advent Songs
Matthew 5:3, 6, 9	35. With Thanksgiving
Matthew 5:3-10	16. Responsive Reading on Psalm 23 and the Beatitudes
Matthew 5:14-16	42. Awake, Rise, and Christ will Shine on You
Matthew 6:21	3. Treasuring God's Wisdom
Matthew 6:22-23	28. A Perceptive Story
Matthew 6:25-33	29. Ask, Seek, Knock
Matthew 6:31-33	35. With Thanksgiving
Matthew 6:33	19. Seek the Lord: Micah and the Prophets
Matthew 6:33	25. Weeds and Harvest
Matthew 7:1-2	25. Weeds and Harvest
Matthew 7:7-8	29. Ask, Seek, Knock
Matthew 7:7-8	35. With Thanksgiving
Matthew 9:35-38	40. Ministry of Reconciliation
Matthew 13:3-9	23. Parable of the Sower
Matthew 13:24-30	25. Weeds and Harvest
Matthew 13:31-33	24. Mystery and Growth
Matthew 13:52	22. What Is New, What Is Old
Matthew 21:5-9	32. Christ as King and Christ as Servant
Matthew 25:31-46	5. If You Do This, You Will Live
Mark 4:26-29	24. Mystery and Growth
Mark 4:26-29	25. Weeds and Harvest
Mark 8:27-33	31. "Who Am I?" The Suffering One, The Transfigured One
Mark 9:2-8	31. "Who Am I?" The Suffering One, The Transfigured One
Mark 10:42-45	32. Christ as King and Christ as Servant
Mark 11:9-10	32. Christ as King and Christ as Servant
Mark 12:28-34	2. With All Your Soul
Mark 12:28-34	3. Treasuring God's Wisdom
Mark 12:41-44	5. If You Do This, You Will Live
Mark 13:33	26. The People Who Walk in Darkness
Mark 14:22-26	43. God Is Our Song
Mark 14:33-36	15. Through the Valley of the Shadow
Luke 1	27. Ancient Advent Songs
Luke 2	27. Ancient Advent Songs
Luke 3:21-22	34. The Spirit of God (Reading 2)
Luke 4:18-19	38. Christ Is Our Peace (Reading 1)
Luke 4:18-21	19. Seek the Lord: Micah and the Prophets
Luke 10:25-28	5. If You Do This, You Will Live
Luke 17:11-19	30. A Thanksgiving Reading
Luke 19:37-40	32. Christ as King and Christ as Servant
Luke 22:24-27	40. Ministry of Reconciliation
Luke 22:26-27	32. Christ as King and Christ as Servant
John 3:8	34. The Spirit of God (Reading 2)

John 4:24	34. The Spirit of God (Reading 2)
John 8:38-39	34. The Spirit of God (Reading 2)
John 9	28. A Perceptive Story
John 13:4-16	32. Christ as King and Christ as Servant
John 14:17, 26	33. The Spirit of God (Reading 1)
John 16:12-13	33. The Spirit of God (Reading 1)
John 20:19-20	33. The Spirit of God (Reading 1)
Acts 2:1-4	34. The Spirit of God (Reading 2)
Romans 5:1-5	15. Through the Valley of the Shadow
Romans 8:28	34. The Spirit of God (Reading 2)
Romans 8:35-39	41. The Breadth and Length and Height and Depth
Romans 11:33	39. Christ Is Our Peace (Reading 2)
Romans 11:33	41. The Breadth and Length and Height and Depth
Romans 12:1-2	7. Bless the Lord, O My Soul
Romans 12:1-2	8. Know and Serve the Lord with Gladness
Romans 12:1-2	37. Present Your Bodies a Living Sacrifice
1 Corinthians 3:10-11	17. What Do These Stones Mean?
1 Corinthians 12:12-26	36. Parable of the Body
2 Corinthians 4:5-6	42. Awake, Rise, and Christ will Shine on You
ä2 Corinthians 4:5-10	9. Declare God's Marvelous Works
2 Corinthians 5:17-20	20. Behold! I Make All Things New!
2 Corinthians 5:17-20	40. Ministry of Reconciliation
Ephesians 2:4-8, 11-22	39. Christ Is Our Peace (Reading 2)
Ephesians 2:11-19	38. Christ Is Our Peace (Reading 1)
Ephesians 3:14-19	2. With All Your Soul
Ephesians 3:14-19	41. The Breadth and Length and Height and Depth
Ephesians 4:14	38. Christ Is Our Peace (Reading 1)
Ephesians 4:14	39. Christ Is Our Peace (Reading 2)
Ephesians 4:14-16	7. Bless the Lord, O My Soul
Ephesians 5:8-9, 14-15	42. Awake, Rise, and Christ will Shine on You
Ephesians 5:15-16	36. Parable of the Body
Philippians 3:12-14	22. What Is New, What Is Old
Philippians 4:6	30. A Thanksgiving Reading
Philippians 4:6, 11-13, 19	35. With Thanksgiving
Philippians 4:8-9	21. A Heart of Wisdom
Colossians 3:9-10, 12-17	37. Present Your Bodies a Living Sacrifice
James 5:7-9	25. Weeds and Harvest
James 3:13-18	23. Parable of the Sower

James 3:17-18   25. Weeds and Harvest

1 Peter 2:4-5, 9-10   9. Declare God's Marvelous Works
1 Peter 2:4-10   17. What Do These Stones Mean?

Revelation 14:1-3   43. God Is Our Song
Revelation 21:1-4   40. Ministry of Reconciliation
Revelation 21:5   20. Behold! I Make All Things New!
Revelation 21:5   38. Christ Is Our Peace (Reading 1)
Revelation 22:1-2   40. Ministry of Reconciliation
Revelation 22:17   34. The Spirit of God (Reading 2)

Hymn Index

Most of the hymns suggested in this book can be found in *Hymnal: A Worship Book* (© 1992 Brethren Press, Faith & Life Press, Mennonite Publishing House). For easy reference, hymns are listed here with the corresponding number in *Hymnal: A Worship Book*. The number in parentheses denotes the readers theater script in this book.

Hymn Title	*Hymnal: A Worship Book*
All Creatures of Our God and King (6)	48
All Hail the Power of Jesus' Name (31, 32)	106, 285
Amazing Grace! (28)	143
Awake, Awake, Fling Off the Night (28, 42)	448
Be Thou My Vision (2, 3, 21, 28)	545
Christ Is Our Cornerstone (17)	43
Come, O Creator Spirit, Come (34)	27
Come, Thou Long-expected Jesus (26, 27)	178
Come Ye Thankful People (25)	94
Create My Soul Anew (7, 37)	3
Earth and All Stars (6, 22)	47
For the Fruit of All Creation (35)	90
For the Healing of the Nations (40)	367
For We Are Strangers No More (38, 39)	322
From the Depths of Sin (13, 14)	136
God Is Working His Purpose Out (23)	638
God of Our Strength (4, 10)	36
God Sends Us the Spirit (34)	293
Gracious Spirit, Dwell with Me (34)	507
Great God of Wonders (39)	149
Great is Thy Faithfulness (10, 22)	327
Guide My Feet (4)	546
Here in This Place (42)	6
Holy, Holy, Holy (7)	75
Holy Spirit, Come with Power (33)	26
I Bind My Heart This Tide (5, 16)	411
If All You Want, Lord (4)	512

If You But Trust in God (11)   576
I Love to Tell the Story (22)   398
Immortal, Invisible, God Only Wise (24)   70
In Christ There Is No East or West (38)   306
I Sought the Lord (3, 8, 13)   506

Joyful, Joyful, We Adore Thee (8)   71
Joy to the World (44)   318

Lead Me, Lord (12, 16, 18)   538
Let All Mortal Flesh Keep Silence (27)   463
Let the Whole Creation Cry (6)   51
Lord, Listen to Your Children (35)   353
Lord of Light, Your Name Outshining (40)   410
Lord, Whose Love in Humble Service (40)   369
Love Divine, All Loves Excelling (41)   592

There Are Many Gifts (36)   304
Mothering God, You Gave Me Birth (22)   482
My Life Flows On (11, 15, 43)   580
My Shepherd Will Supply My Need (16)   589
My Soul Proclaims with Wonder (27)   181

New Earth, Heavens New (20, 22)   299

O Come, O Come, Immanuel (27)   172
O God, in Restless Living (29)   557
O God, Our Help in Ages Past (22)   328
Oh, That I Had a Thousand Voices (9)   84
O Little Town of Bethlehem (27)   191
O Love That Will Not Let Me Go (13, 41)   577
O Power of Love (41)   593
O Praise the Gracious Power (38, 39)   111

Praise, I Will Praise You, Lord (1, 9)   76
Praise, My Soul, the God of Heaven! (2)   63
Praise, My Soul, the King of Heaven! (7, 14)   65
Precious Lord, Take My Hand (15)   575

Seed, Scattered and Sown (23)   454
Seek Ye First the Kingdom of God (29)   324
Shepherd Me, O God (15, 16)   519
Sing Praise to God Who Reigns (19, 43)   59
Sing to the Lord of Harvest (25, 35)   98
Sleepers, Wake! (42)   188
Sometimes a Light Surprises (29)   603

Teach Me Thy Truth (8)   548
The Church's One Foundation (17)   311
The King of Love My Shepherd Is (16)   170
The Kingdom of God (24)   224
There's a Wideness in God's Mercy (25)   145
The Work is Thine, O Christ (40)   396
They That Wait Upon the Lord (10)   584
This Is a Day of New Beginnings (22)   640
Thou True Vine, That Heals (23)   373

Veni Sancte Spiritus (34)   298

We Are People of God's Peace (38)   407
We Give Thanks unto You (1)   161
We Plow the Fields and Scatter (23)   96
We Would Extol Thee (3)   74
What Does the Lord Require? (18)   409
What Mercy and Divine Compassion (39)   524
When All Thy Mercies, O My God (7, 35)   72
When in Our Music God is Glorified (43)   44
When I Survey the Wondrous Cross (31)   259
When Peace, Like a River (2)   336
Will You Let Me Be Your Servant? (32)   307
You Are Salt for the Earth (16, 23)   226

Put JOY, EXCITEMENT, AND PRAISE in Your Worship Experiences

Let All Within Us Praise!
Songs for Worship and Celebration
by Patricia J. Shelly

Let All Within Us Praise! Songs for Worship and Celebration is a plea to bring the full range of human emotion into our worship. Patricia Shelly—a gifted musician, pastor, scholar, and worship leader—has created these songs to strengthen and deepen the worship experience.

Using a comfortable musical style that is at home in both contemporary and traditional worship, Patricia Shelly's songs communicate well with youth and adults alike. *Let All Within Us Praise! Songs for Worship and Celebration* can be used in many settings, from camps and spiritual retreats to congregational worship.

Sixteen Scripture-based songs—all with chord symbols and many with full piano accompaniment—offer a variety of ways to express and proclaim God's Word.

Songs included:

Love the Lord (With All)
Many Gifts
Micah
Philippine Hymn
Love Suffers Much
Prayer for Peace

Jerusalem
Joy Wasn't in Me
The Light Shines in the Darkness
Communion Song
Benediction
and others

This songbook contains the sixteen songs included in Patricia Shelly's ***Let All Within Us Praise! Dramatic Resources for Worship*** published by Faith & Life Press.

ISBN 0-87303-209-8, $4.95 U.S. / $6.95 CAN

 FAITH & LIFE PRESS · 718 MAIN · P.O. BOX 347 · NEWTON, KS 67114-0347
FAITH & LIFE PRESS CANADA · 600 SHAFTESBURY BLVD. · WINNIPEG, MB R3P 0M4

------✄-- Order Form ----------

Let All Within Us Praise! Songs for Worship and Celebration

Please send _____ *Let All Within Us Praise! songbook* at $4.95 U.S./$6.95 CAN $_____

Kansas customers add 5.9% sales tax $_____

Canadian customers add 7% GST $_____

Shipping (please add $3.00 for 1 book; $ .50 for each add'l book) $_____

Check enclosed for TOTAL $_____

Name_____

Address_____

City _____ State/Prov. _____ Postal Code _____

To order: **Call the toll-free Faith & Life OrderLine:**   **1 800 743-2484**

Or you may order from your local bookstore.

Or return this order form to Faith & Life Press, Newton or Winnipeg.